# Women in Christian History

## A Bibliography

# Women in Christian History

## A Bibliography

compiled and edited by
### Carolyn DeArmond Blevins

### MERCER
1995

ISBN 0-86554-493-X                                        MUP/H387


*Women in Christian History. A Bibliography.*
Copyright ©1995
Mercer University Press, Macon, Georgia 31210-3960
All rights reserved
Printed in the United States of America
First printing, October 1995


♠


The paper used in this publication meets the minimum requirements
of American National Standard for Information Sciences—
Permanence of Paper for Printed Library Materials,
ANSI Z39.48-1984.


♠


*Library of Congress Cataloging-in-Publication Data*

Blevins, Carolyn DeArmond, 1936–
Women in Christian history : a bibliography /
compiled and edited by Carolyn DeArmond Blevins
x+114pp. 6x9" (15x23cm.).
Includes index.
ISBN 0-86554-493-X (alk. paper).
1. Church history—Bibliography.
2. Women in Christianity—History—Bibliography.
I. Title.
Z7963.R45B45      1995
[BV639.W7]
270'.082—dc20      95-24835                             CIP

# Contents

Preface . . . . . . . . . . . . . . . . . . . . . . . . . . . . . . . . . . . . . . . . . . .  vii

Women in Christian History. A Bibliography  . . . . . . . . . . . .  1-110

General Reference  . . . . . . . . . . . . . . . . . . . . . . . . . . . . . . . . .  1

Historical Periods  . . . . . . . . . . . . . . . . . . . . . . . . . . . . . . . .  5
   Historiography  . . . . . . . . . . . . . . . . . . . . . . . . . . . . . . . .  5
   General History . . . . . . . . . . . . . . . . . . . . . . . . . . . . . . . .  5
   Early Christianity  . . . . . . . . . . . . . . . . . . . . . . . . . . . . .  17
   Medieval Period  . . . . . . . . . . . . . . . . . . . . . . . . . . . . . . .  24
   Reformation Period  . . . . . . . . . . . . . . . . . . . . . . . . . . . . .  35
   Europe: Modern Period  . . . . . . . . . . . . . . . . . . . . . . . . . .  39
   America: General History  . . . . . . . . . . . . . . . . . . . . . . . .  40
   America: Colonial Period  . . . . . . . . . . . . . . . . . . . . . . . .  44
   America: Nineteenth Century  . . . . . . . . . . . . . . . . . . . . .  49
   America: Twentieth Century  . . . . . . . . . . . . . . . . . . . . . .  56

Ethnic and/or National Groups  . . . . . . . . . . . . . . . . . . . . . .  61
   Africa . . . . . . . . . . . . . . . . . . . . . . . . . . . . . . . . . . . . . . . .  61
   African-American . . . . . . . . . . . . . . . . . . . . . . . . . . . . . . .  61
   Asian  . . . . . . . . . . . . . . . . . . . . . . . . . . . . . . . . . . . . . . . .  66
   British  . . . . . . . . . . . . . . . . . . . . . . . . . . . . . . . . . . . . . . .  66
   Hispanic . . . . . . . . . . . . . . . . . . . . . . . . . . . . . . . . . . . . . .  71
   Native American  . . . . . . . . . . . . . . . . . . . . . . . . . . . . . . . .  71

Denominations and/or Sects  . . . . . . . . . . . . . . . . . . . . . . . . .  72
   Baptist  . . . . . . . . . . . . . . . . . . . . . . . . . . . . . . . . . . . . . . .  72
   Catholic  . . . . . . . . . . . . . . . . . . . . . . . . . . . . . . . . . . . . . .  75
   Christian Reformed  . . . . . . . . . . . . . . . . . . . . . . . . . . . . .  79
   Christian Science  . . . . . . . . . . . . . . . . . . . . . . . . . . . . . . .  80

Church of the Brethren ......................... 81
Church of God ................................. 82
Congregational ................................ 82
Disciples of Christ ............................. 83
Eastern Orthodox .............................. 83
Episcopal ...................................... 83
Jehovah's Witness .............................. 85
Lutheran ...................................... 85
Mennonite .................................... 86
Methodist ..................................... 86
Moravian ...................................... 94
Mormon ....................................... 95
Oneida Community ............................. 96
Pentecostal .................................... 96
Presbyterian ................................... 97
Quaker ........................................ 99
Seventh-Day Adventist ......................... 102
Shakers ....................................... 103
Unitarian (*see also* Universalist) .................. 105
United Brethren ............................... 106
Universalist (*see also* Unitarian) .................. 106

Hymn Writers ................................. 107

Social Reform/Social Work ........................ 107

Index of Names ................................. 111

# Preface

One of the distinctive features of Jesus' ministry was the involvement of women. Yet the traditional story of developing Christianity curiously omitted the roles and contributions of women. Women's studies programs emerged in the 1970s and attempted to bring into focus the story of women in Christian history. Specific courses focused on women's experience in Christianity.

By the 1980s some historians and feminists encouraged teachers to move away from women's studies courses and incorporate the women's story into their traditional history courses. Carolyn Plampin, a retired missionary teacher, realized that more teachers could include material on women's role in Christianity if those teachers had a bibliography to help them do so. She dreamed of recruiting people to develop bibliographies in various subjects to encourage college and graduate faculty to include women's story in their courses. Plampin asked the Baptist Women in Ministry group to sponsor this long-range project which they agreed to do. Plampin enlisted me to compile the bibliography on Women in Church History, sending me some preliminary research she had done.

Every month it seemed the project grew. The more sources I found, the more I discovered to research. A bibliography is never complete because materials are overlooked or are difficult to obtain, and continue to be published. A dedicated attempt to diminish each of these problems has been made, but there are still omissions.

Each item listed has been examined by me. Materials were located in college, university, and theological school libraries, and through interlibrary loans. Still some materials were not located, and since one of the criteria for inclusion was availability, regrettably those items are not included.

Other criteria besides availability that governed the selections in this bibliography are historical emphasis, primary material, and documentation. A few exceptions were made. Some literature is included when it reflects writings of significant religious figures. A few items of a biblical nature are listed when they reflect a particular group's viewpoint. Obviously entries on education and social issues could be numerous since those two fields often are frequently related to religious groups or causes. Only a few are included here. Generally materials written a century or more ago are not included unless they have been reprinted, since accessibility is otherwise limited. Documentation notes are included with many entries to alert the user to the item's value in research or in locating other sources.

Entries are arranged by broad topics. Cross-references are included where significant material appears in a source listed elsewhere. The name index will provide additional assistance for quick referencing.

An effort of this size is not a solitary project. I am indebted to those who have birthed it with me. Carolyn Plampin conceived the project and continued to nurture it. George Anna Self, Carson-Newman College circulation librarian, diligently chased many books through interlibrary loan. My husband Bill assisted me in checking card catalogs and was my ceaseless encourager. Kym, our youngest daughter, entered data into the computer. To each I owe much thanks. ▲

7 August 1995                                    *Carolyn DeArmond Blevins*

❧

Dedicated
to
three generations of women in my family
Ruth
Suzanne and Kym
Alex, Jaclyn, and Sydney

❧

# A Bibliography

## General Reference

Ballou, Patricia K. *Women: A Bibliography of Bibliographies.* Boston: G. K. Hall, 1980. 155 pp. Personal name index.
Includes a small section on women in Christianity.

Bass, Dorothy. *American Women in Church and Society: 1607–1920; a Bibliography.* New York: Union Theological Seminary, 1973. 36 pp. Annotated. Contains a brief section on religion.
Very useful for 19th and early 20th century.

Brunkow, Robert, ed. *Religion and Society in North America: An Annotated Bibliography.* Santa Barbara CA: ABC-Clio Information Services, 1983. 515 pp. Includes valuable subject index.

Conway, Jill K. *The Female Experience in Eighteenth- and Nineteenth-Century America: A Guide to the History of American Women.* New York: Garland Publishing Co., 1982. 290 pp.
Includes bibliographic essay on "Women Missionaries, Religious, and Evangelists of the Early National Period" and a significant section on "Women's Religious Life and the Reform Tradition, 1790–1860," which includes discussions of women's contributions to the antislavery movement, millennial communities, perfected societies, Mormonism, and Unitarianism.

Een, JoAnn Delores, and Marie B. Rosenbery-Dishman. *Women and Society: Citations 3601-6000.* Beverly Hills CA and London: Sage Publications, 1978.
Includes a short section on women in philosophy and religion.

Eltscher, Susan M. *Women in the Wesleyan and United Methodist Traditions: A Bibliography.* Madison NJ: General Commission on Archives and History, United Methodist Church, 1992. 158 pp. Extensive listing by topics, good index.

Farians, Elizabeth. *Selected Bibliography on Women and Religion.* N.p., 1971.

Hammack, Mary L. *A Dictionary of Women in Church History.* Chicago: Moody Press, 1984. 167 pp. General bibliography provided; no references provided with individual entries. Indexed according to periods in church history.
   Useful for identifying individual women.

Harrison, Cynthia, Anne Firor Scott, and Pamela R. Byrne. *Women in American History: A Bibliography.* Santa Barbara CA and Oxford, England: Clio Press, 1979. 373 pp. Includes subject and author indexes.
   Valuable abstracts of articles in 550 periodicals, many related to women in Christianity.

⌐ James, Edward T., Janet Wilson James, and Paul S. Boyer, eds. *Notable American Women: A Biographical Dictionary 1607–1950.* 3 vols. Cambridge MA: Harvard University Press, 1971. Bibliographic references provided.
   Excellent resource. Vol. 3 contains a classified listing that includes educators, ministers and evangelists, missionaries, mission society leaders, religious educators, religious founders and leaders. *See* Sicherman and Green for *Notable American Women: The Modern Period.* Cambridge MA: Harvard University Press, 1980.

Klejment, Anne and Alice. *Dorothy Day and "The Catholic Worker": A Bibliography and Index..* New York: Garland Publishing, 1986. 412 pp. Includes a bibliography of works by Day, a bibliography about Day and the newspaper, and four indexes.
   Valuable resource.

Kolmer, Elizabeth. "Catholic Women Religious and Women's History: A Survey of the Literature." In *Women in American Religion,* by Janet

Wilson James, 127-39. Philadelphia: University of Pennsylvania Press, 1980.
  A very useful bibliography.

Kolmer, Elizabeth. *Religious Women in the United States: A Survey of the Influential Literature from 1950–1983.* Wilmington DE: Michael Glazier, 1984. 111 pp.
  Primarily Roman Catholic. Seventy pages of a survey of literature, 27 pages of bibliographic listings.

McDowell, Barbara, and Hana Umlauf, eds. *Woman's Almanac.* New York: Newspaper Enterprise Association, 1977.
  See "Spiritual Women," 393-408. Some background articles and brief accounts of women. Of limited value.

Parbury, Kathleen. *Women of Grace: A Biographical Dictionary of British Women Saints, Martyrs, and Reformers.* Boston: Oriel Press, 1985. 199 pp. Brief bibliography.
  Includes women from early times to 1845. Predominantly Catholic. Includes a substantial dictionary of monastic houses for women.

Patrick, Anne E. "Women and Religion: A Survey of Significant Literature, 1965–1974." *Theological Studies* 36/4 (1975): 737-65. Also in *Woman: New Dimensions* edited by Walter Burkhardt.
  Dated but still valuable. Good bibliographic essay that includes historical literature.

*Religious Books, 1876–1982.* New York: R. W. Bowker Co., 1983. Vol. 3 includes women in Christianity. Brief annotations. Citations for various denominations.

Richardson, Marilyn. *Black Women and Religion, a Bibliography.* Boston: G. K. Hall, 1980. 139 pp. Index.
  Valuable annotations. Introductory essay on three women: Jarena Lee, Maria Steward, and Anna Julia Cooper. Sections devoted to books and articles, literature, music, art, audiovisual materials, and reference materials. Appendix includes a list of autobiographies and biographies as well as 17 biographical sketches.

Robbins, Russell H. *The Encyclopedia of Witchcraft and Demonology.* New York: Crown Publishers, 1959. 571 pp. Includes bibliography.
Fine, substantial resource.

Rowe, Kenneth E. *Methodist Women: a Guide to the Literature.* Lake Junaluska NC: General Commission on Archives and History, United Methodist Church, 1980. 50 pp. Author index.
British and American works are the focus.

Sicherman, Barbara, and Carol Hurd Green, eds. *Notable American Women. The Modern Period. A Biographical Dictionary.* Cambridge MA: Harvard University Press, 1980.
    Excellent resource. Covers years of late-nineteeth century to mid-20th century. Entries include bibliographic references. A classified listing of the biographies includes religion. *See above*, James, James, and Boyer, *Notable American Women 1607–1950.*

Smith, William. *A Dictionary of Christian Biography, Literature, Sects, and Doctrines; Being a Continuation of "The Dictionary of the Bible."* 4 vols. London: J. Murray, 1877–1887.
Old but useful.

Szasz, Ferenc. "An Annotated Bibliography of Women in American Religious History: The Christian Tradition, 1607–1900." *Iliff Review* 40/3 (1983): 41-59.

Thomas, Evangeline, ed. *Women Religious History Sources: A Guide to Repositories in the United States.* New York: R. W. Bowker Co., 1983. 329 pp.

White, Ellen G. *Comprehensive Index to the Writings of Ellen G. White.* 3 vols. Mountain View CA: Pacific Press, 1962. More than 3,000 pp. Three indexes (scripture, topical, and quotations) of her writings printed by 1958. Very useful appendixes. Topical index comprises the major portion of the volumes.

# Historical Periods

## Historiography

Lerner, Gerda. *Teaching Women's History.* Washington DC: American Historical Association, 1981. 88 pp. A lengthy and valuable bibliography.

Useful suggestions for incorporating women's story into traditional histories. See esp. the sections on "Women in Religious Life," "The Uses of Autobiography and Biography," and the various sections on women in selected ethnic groups.

## General History

Anderson, Bonnie S., and Judith P. Zinsser. *A History of Their Own: Women in Europe from Prehistory to the Present.* 2 vols. New York: Harper & Row, 1988.

In vol. 1, see esp. "The Effects of Christianity" (67-84; on beliefs and practices empowering or subordinating women), and the section on "Women and the Churches: The Power of the Faithful": "Authority within the Institutional Church" (183-213); "Authority outside the Institutional Church" (214-27); and "Traditional Images Redrawn" (253-63). Vol. 2 provides valuable social and political background.

Bliss, Kathleen. *The Service and Status of Women in the Churches.* London: SCM Press, 1954. 208 pp. Undocumented; index.

Based on information from fifty countries in the early 1950s, Bliss examines the function and status of women in churches associated with the World Council of Churches. Focuses on voluntary service, professional service, ordained ministry, and participation in church goverance.

Bloom, Naomi. *Contributions of Women: Religion.* Minneapolis: Dillon Press, 1978. 128 pp.

Easily read accounts of Anne Hutchinson, Ann Lee, Mary Baker Eddy, and Dorothy Day. Brief sketches of other women included.

Bowie, Fiona, Deborah Kirkwood, and Shirley Ardener. *Women and Missions: Past and Present Anthropological and Historical Perceptions.*

Providence RI and Oxford, England: Berg Publishers, 1993. 279 pp. Includes three indexes.
    Thirteen essays examining women's impact on missions and the impact of missions on women.

Bowie, Walter Russell. *Women of Light*. New York: Harper & Row, 1968. 205 pp. Includes bibliographic references.
    Brief biographical sketches, including Joan of Arc and Susanna Wesley.

Brunner, Peter. *The Ministry and the Ministry of Women*. St. Louis: Concordia Publishing House, 1971. 39 pp.
    Women as ministers and volunteers in the church.

Bullough, Vern L. with Bonnie Bullough. *The Subordinate Sex, A History of Attitudes toward Women*. Urbana: University of Illinois Press, 1976. 375 pp. Annotated bibliography.
    Assesses attitudes of Eastern and Western Christianity. One chapter focuses on America.

Byrne, Lavina, ed. *The Hidden Tradition: Women's Spiritual Writings Rediscovered: An Anthology*. London: SPCK, 1991. 198 pp. Includes biographical notes, bibliography.
    A fine collection of primary materials written by women throughout Christian history. The material is organized around broad themes and ranges from Balthilda to Dorothy Sayers.

Caro Baroja, Julio. *The World of Witches*. Chicago: University of Chicago Press, 1964. 313 pp.
    Historical examination of witchcraft from Graeco-Roman times to modern interpretations.

Christ, Carol P. "Heretics and Outsiders: The Struggle Over Female Power in Western Religion." *Soundings* 61 (Fall 1978): 260-79.
    Traces the struggle from ancient Hebrew religions to the current setting. Good documentation.

Clark, Elizabeth A., and Herbert Richardson, eds. *Women and Religion: A Feminist Sourcebook of Christian Thought.* New York: Harper & Row, 1977. 298 pp. Good documentation.

Introduction is an excellent survey of women in religion. Fine collection of documents by both men and women from the Greek period to the 1970s, including Clement of Alexandria, Jerome, Augustine, Aquinas, Julian of Norwich, Margery Kempe, *Malleus Maleficarum,* Luther, Milton, Ann Lee, Schleiermacher, Baader, Noyes, Grimke, Stanton, *The Casti Connubi,* Barth, and Daly.

Code, Joseph B. *Great American Foundresses.* Freeport NY: Books for Libraries Press, 1968. 502 pp. No bibliography, but a good index.

Examines lives of sixteen women who founded religious communities in the United States.

Coon, Lynda L. Katherine J. Haldane and Elisabeth W. Sommer. *That Gentle Strength: Historical Perspectives on Women in Christianity.* Charlottesville: University Press of Virginia, 1990. 267 pp. Includes bibliographic references, index.

Essays chronicling the conflicts, struggles, and achievements of women in Christianity.

Culver, Elsie Thomas. *Women in the World of Religion.* Garden City NY: Doubleday and Co., 1967. 340 pp. Includes bibliographic references, index.

Includes chapters on the early church; service opportunities; contributions of women during the medieval, Renaissance, and Reformation periods; witches; puritans; pietists; Methodists; missions; suffrage, abolition, temperance causes; cults; YWCA; in her church; church councils; preaching, teaching and other occupations; and contemporary status.

Davis, Elizabeth Gould. *The First Sex.* New York: G. P. Putnam's Sons, 1971. 382 pp. Includes bibliographic references.

Chapters 14-20 examine attitudes toward women from early Christianity to the present and notes roles of selected women.

Dayton, Donald W. *Discovering an Evangelical Heritage.* Peabody MA: Hendrickson Publishers, 1976.

Includes a chapter on "The Evangelical Roots of Feminism" (85-98), a good discussion of individuals and movements within evangelicalism that gave birth to feminism.

Dayton, Donald W., and Lucille Sider Dayton. "Women as Preachers: Evangelical Precedents." *Christianity Today* (23 May 1975): 4-7.
Concise historical account of women preachers in the United States from the 18th century to the present.

Deen, Edith. *Great Women of the Christian Faith*. New York: Harper & Row, 1959. 410 pp. Undocumented, but includes bibliography and index.
Biographical sketches of 45 women from the 2nd century to the 20th. Vignettes of 77 additional women. Some conjecture blended with facts. A useful survey.

Duby, George L., and Michelle Perrot, eds. *A History of Women in the West*. 4 vols. Cambridge MA: Harvard University Press, 1992, 1993.
See esp., in vol. 1, "Religious Roles of Roman Women" (377-408) and "Early Christian Women" (409-44). In vol. 2 (also Klapisch-Zuber under Medieval Period, below), see "The Clerical Gaze" by Jacques Dalarun (15-42). In vol. 3, see "Virgins and Mothers between Heaven and Earth" by Elisja Schulte van Kessel (132-66); and "Witches" by Jean-Michel Sallmann (444-57). In vol. 4, see "The Catholic Model" by Michela De Giorgio (166-97); "The Protestant Woman" by Jean Bauberot (198-212); "The New Eve and the Old Adam" by Annelise Maugue (515-32).

Ermarth, Margaret Sittler. *Adam's Fractured Rib*. Philadelphia: Fortress Press, 1970. 159 pp. Includes short bibliography.
Includes excerpts from primary materials. Examines briefly the experience of women in the Roman Catholic, Greek Orthodox, Anglican, United Presbyterian, United Methodist, American Baptist, United Church of Christ, Church of the Brethren, and Lutheran churches, and churches in Switzerland, France, Germany, Scandinavia, and India. Heaviest emphasis is on Lutheranism.

Falk, Nancy A., and Rita M. Gross. *Unspoken Worlds: Women's Religious Lives.* Belmont CA: Wadsworth Publishing. 1989. 284 pp. Includes bibliography.
  Includes articles on Dorothy Day and women's power in the church, the roles of women in Sunday Schools, and women in the Shaker tradition.

Fink, R. A. "Women in the Church." *Quarterly Review of the Evangelical Lutheran Church* (April 1874): 220-33.
  Regarding restricted roles based on Bible.

Foster, Warren Dunham, ed. *Heroines of Modern Religion.* Freeport NY: Books for Libraries Press, 1970. Reprint of 1913 edition. 275 pp. Includes bibliography, chronological outline, index.
  Includes Anne Hutchinson, Susanna Wesley, Elizabeth Ann Seton, Lucretia Mott, Fanny Crosby, Sister Dora, Hannah Whitall Smith, Frances Ridley Havergal, Ramabai Dongre Medlavi, and Maud Ballington Booth.

Fraser, Dorothy Bass. "Women with a Past: A New Look at the History of Theological Education." *Theological Education* 8 (Summer 1972).

Golder, C. *History of the Deaconess Movement in the Christian Church.* Cincinnati: Jennings and Pye, 1903. 614 pp. Undocumented, but includes statistical tables and index.
  Traces deaconesses from Apostolic times, through various European movements, and in several denominations in America. Appendix contains several documents relating to deaconesses.

Hardesty, Nancy A. *Great Women of Faith: The Strength and Influence of Christian Women.* Grand Rapids: Baker Book House, 1980. 140 pp. Selected bibliography.
  Biographical sketches of 26 women from the 4th century to the 20th. Predominantly European and American, although Ramabai of India is also included. Reading suggestions are grouped according to individual women.

Harkness, Georgia Elma. *Women in Church and Society: A Historical and Theological Inquiry.* Nashville: Abingdon Press, 1972. 240 pp. Good documentation, index.

Provides a succinct survey of the role of women in Christianity, biblical models, and contemporary issues.

Harris, Louise. *Woman in the Christian Church.* Brighton MI: Green Oak Press. 1988. 200 pp. Good documentation, index.

Includes historical overview, discussions of specific women and reports of various eccesiological responses to ordination. Appendix identifies distinguished women.

Hassey, Janette. *No Time for Silence: Evangelical Women in Public Ministry Around the Turn of the Century.* Grand Rapids: Zondervan, 1986. 254 pp. Excellent documentation, thirteen appendixes, bibliography, and subject and scripture indexes.

Chronicles the significant ways women were involved in Christian ministry before Fundamentalism stifled their opportunities.

Hinson, E. Glenn. *The Church Triumphant. A History of Christianity up to 1300.* Macon GA: Mercer University Press, 1995. xxii+494 pp. Integrates well the story of women.

Ide, Arthur Frederick. *Sex, Woman, and Religion.* Woman in History series 100. Dallas: Monument Press, 1984. 215 pp. Index.

Chapters on woman in early Christianity, Byzantine woman, woman in Europe's middle years, and modern woman are of limited value.

Johnson, Suzan D., ed. *Wise Women Bearing Gifts: Joys and Struggles of Their Faith.* Valley Forge PA: Judson Press, 1988. 92 pp. No documentation.

The stories of fifteen women ministers, clergy and lay. African-American, Puerto Rican, Native American, and caucasian women are included.

Kaplan, Justin. *With Malice toward Women: A Handbook for Women-Haters Drawn from the Best Minds of All Time.* New York: Dodd, Mead, 1952. 255 pp.

Includes the writings of Jerome, Tertullian, John Knox, Nietzsche, and a section of writings on witches. "The most formidable of all the organized campaigns against women was the one conducted by the church for nearly a thousand years. For celibacy to be glorified, woman had to be damned."

King, Margor. *The Desert Mothers: A Survey of the Feminine Anchoretic Tradition in Western Europe.* Saskatoon, Saskatchewan, 1985. 38 pp. Includes fine notes.

Kittredge, George Lyman. *Witchcraft in Old and New England.* New York: Russell and Russell, 1956. 641 pp. Extensive documentation, bibliography, and index.

Knox, John. *The Works of John Knox.* Vol. 4. Edited by David Laing. New York: AMS Press, 1966.
    See "The First Blast of the Trumpet against the Monstrous Regiment of Women, 1558" (349-422).

Kraemer, Ross S. "The Conversion of Women to Ascetic Forms of Christianity." *Signs* 6 (Winter 1980): 298-307. Good documentation.

Langdon-Davies, John. *A Short History of Women.* New York: Literary Guild of America, 1927. 382 pp.
    An interesting pro-woman stance from the 1920s. Traces history from the primitive to the modern eras, charting the tensions between women, society, and Christianity.

MacHaffie, Barbara J. *Her Story: Women in Christian Tradition.* Philadelphia: Fortress Press, 1986. 184 pp. Well documented, extensive suggested readings, subject index, and scripture index.
    Concise survey of the images, roles, contributions, and impact of women in Christianity, showing women to be neither "passive nor powerless."

_____. *Readings in Her Story: Women in Christian History.* Minneapolis: Fortress Press, 1992. 238 pp.

Superb collection of readings. Well-chosen readings from each era: nine from the early church years, eight from the medieval period, eight from the Reformation era, eight from the American colonies, seven related to mission and reform movements, six on 19th-century preachers and scholars, seven related to Catholicism and sectarianism, six examining the status of women in mainline denominations, and six dealing with recent feminist issues.

McPhee, Carol, and Ann FitzGerald, compilers. *Feminist Quotations: Voices of Rebels, Reformers, and Visionaries.* New York: Thomas Y. Crowell, 1979. 271 pp. Indexes.

The section on religion (124-30) includes quotations from women on the subject of religion.

Martindale, C. C. *The Queen's Daughters: A Study of Women-Saints.* New York: Sheed and Ward, 1951. 207 pp. No sources, index.

Discusses saints from the 2nd century to the early 20th.

Mayeski, Marie Anne. *Women: Models of Liberation.* Kansas City: Sheed and Ward, 1988. 240 pp. Includes documentation, bibliography.

Introduces the writer, suggests feminist interpretations of her writings, provides excerpts from her writings. Writers included are Perpetua, Heloise, Julian of Norwich, Teresa of Avila, Sister Blandina Segale, and Caryll Houselander.

Miles, Margaret Ruth. *Carnal Knowing: Female Nakedness and Religious Meaning in the Christian West.* Boston: Beacon Press, 1989. 254 pp. Large bibliography, index.

See "'Becoming Male': Women Marytrs and Ascetics" (53-77).

O'Faolain, Julia, and Lauro Martines, eds. *Not in God's Image, Women in History from the Greeks to the Victorians.* New York: Harper & Row, 1973. 362 pp. Good documentation, brief bibliography, source index, subject index.

Excerpts from primary documents of various eras and cultures. Note esp. "The Christian Context," "Education and Religion," "Protestants," "Witches," and "The Protestant Promotion of Women."

Olson, Jeannine E. *One Ministry, Many Roles: Deacons and Deaconesses through the Centuries.* St. Louis: Concordia Publishing House, 1992. 460 pp. Well documented, large bibliography, large index.

Traces roles and work of deaconesses from early church to 20th century in Europe and America.

Pate, Billie. "Birth and Rebirth of Feminism: Responses of Church Women." *Review and Expositor* 72 (Winter 1975): 53-61. Good documentation.

Porterfield, Amanda. *Feminine Spirituality in America: From Sarah Edwards to Martha Graham.* Philadelphia: Temple University Press, 1980. 238 pp. Includes bibliographic references, index.

Porterfield, E. Amanda. "Maidens, Missionaries and Mothers: American Women as Subjects and Objects of Religiousness." Ph.D. dissertation, Stanford University, 1975. 203 pp.

Explores allusions to femininity: "Women and Puritan Spirituality—the Sacrality of Marriage," "Effeminate Pietists and Masculine Rationalists," "The World Is a Home," "The Home Is a World," and "Feminine Sexuality as Religious Evil."

Putlick, Elizabeth, and Peter B. Clark, eds. *Women as Teachers and Disciples in Traditional and New Religions.* Studies in Women and Religion 32. Lewiston NY: Edwin Mellen Press, 1993. 146 pp. Index.

Ten essays. See esp. "Desert Mothers: Women Ascetics in Early Christian Egypt."

Rothman, Sheila. *Woman's Proper Place: A History of Changing Ideals and Practices, 1870 to the Present.* New York: Basic Books, 1978. 322 pp. Well documented, index.

See chapter on "The Protestant Nun."

Ruether, Rosemary Radford, and Eleanor McLaughlin. *Women of Spirit: Female Leadership in the Jewish and Christian Traditions.* New York: Simon & Schuster, 1979. 400 pp. Good documentation, index.

Fourteen essays that focus on women's experience in early Christian communities, the Patristic Age, medieval Christianity, the Counter-

Reformation, as Quakers in the English left wing, as female mystics, in sectarian Christianity, in the Holiness movement, as American nuns, in antebellum America, as American Protestants, in Judaism, as Episcopalians, and as Roman Catholics.

Russell, Jeffrey Burton. *A History of Witchcraft: Sorcerers, Heretics, and Pagans.* New York: Thames and Hudson, 1980. 192 pp. Well documented, includes 94 good illustrations, bibliography, index.
    Examines several aspects of the rise of witchcraft.

Schneir, Miriam, compiler. *Feminism: The Essential Historical Writings.* New York: Random House, 1972.
    Includes Sojourner Truth's "Ain't I a Woman?" and Lucretia Mott's "Not Christianity but Priestcraft."

Sheils, W. J., and Diana Woods, eds. *Women in the Church.* Studies in Church History 27. Oxford: Basil Blackwell, 1990. 515 pp. No bibliography, no index.
    Thirty-one papers read at the 1989 summer meeting and 1990 winter meeting of the Ecclesiastical History Society. Topics range from women who worked within the institutions to those who refused to obey it. The papers span the periods from the Church Fathers to the 20th century.

Smith, Betsy Covington. *Breakthrough: Women in Religion.* New York: Walker and Co., 1978. 139 pp. Glossary; no documentation, bibliography, or index.
    Stories of five ordained women leaders: Jeannette Piccard, Episcopal; Rabbi Sandy Sasso; Sister Joques Egan, Catholic; Patricia Green, A.M.E; Daphne Hawkes, Episcopal.

Smith-Rosenberg, Carroll. "Women and Religious Revivals: Antiritualism, Liminality, and the Emergence of the American Bourgeoisie," in *The Evangelical Tradition in America,* ed. Leonard I. Sweet, 199-231. Macon GA: Mercer University Press, 1984.

Thomas, Keith. *Religion and the Decline of Magic.* New York: Charles Scribner's Sons, 1971. 716 pp. Well documented, excellent index.

A fine section on witchcraft (435-583), the crime, its history, its relationship to religion, "the making of a witch," the social environment, and its decline.

Todd, Margo. "Humanists, Puritans, and the Spiritualized Household." *Christian History* 49 (March 1980): 18-34. Well documented.

Torrey, Charles W. "Woman's Sphere in the Church" in *Congregational Quarterly* (April 1867): 163-71.
Opposes leadership.

Tucker, Ruth A. *Guardians of the Great Commission: A History of Women in Modern Missions.* Grand Rapids: Zondervan Publishing House, 1988. 278 pp. Documented, bibliography, index.
Brief accounts of the involvement of 63 women in diverse areas of missions in the 19th and 20th centuries.

Tucker, Ruth A., and Walter L. Liefeld. *Daughters of the Church: Women and Ministry from New Testament Times to the Present.* Grand Rapids: Zondervan Publishing House, 1987. 552 pp. Thorough documentation, valuable appendixes, extensive bibliography, subject index, scripture index.
An account of woman's experience in Christianity weaving individual stories with topical studies. Note esp. the following chapters: "The Rise of the Church and the Downfall of Rome"; "Medieval Catholicism"; "Reformation Protestantism"; "Post-Reformation Sectarianism"; "Transatlantic Reform and Revivalism"; "Foreign Missions"; "The Non-Western Church"; and "Modern Pentecostalism and Denominationalism"

Tucker, Ruth A. *First Ladies of the Parish: Historical Portraits of Pastors' Wives.* Grand Rapids: Zondervan, 1988. 204 pp. Good documentation, bibliography, index.
Brief biographical sketches of Katie Luther, Katherine Zell, Idelette Calvin, Susanna Wesley, Mary Fletcher, Sarah Edwards, Eunice Beecher, Margaret Simpson, Susannah Spurgeon, Emma Moody, Daisy Smith, Catherine Marshall, Ruth Peale, Jill Briscoe.

Turpin, Joanne. *Women in Church History: Twenty Stories for Twenty Centuries.* Cincinnati OH: St. Anthony Messenger Press, 1990. 173 pp. A historical sketch of one woman in each century.

Van Vuuren, Nancy. *The Subversion of Women: As Practiced by Churches, Witch Hunters, and other Sexists.* Philadelphia: Westminster Press, 1973. 190 pp. Includes bibliography.

Three major sections on the subjugation of women in the Judeo-Christian tradition, witchcraft as a threat to church and state supremacy, and sex as a self-destructive weapon. Includes "The Bull of Innocent VIII."

Webster, John C. B., and Ellen Low. *The Church and Women in the Third World.* Philadelphia: Westminster Press, 1985. 167 pp. Includes bibliography.

Focuses on experiences in China, India, Latin America, Africa, and Philippians.

Wessinger, Catherine, ed. *Women's Leadership in Marginal Religions: Explorations outside the Mainstream.* Urbana and Chicago: University of Illnois Press, 1993. 246 pp. Well documented, index.

Twelve essays include discussions of women in the Shakers, Pentecostal, Christian Science Theosophical Movement, African American spiritual churches in New Orleans, and discussions of Emma Curtis Hopkins, and Myrtle Fillmore.

Williams, Charles. *Witchcraft.* New York: Meridian Books, 1959. 316 pp. Historical account from the Dark Ages to Salem.

Williamson, Claude Charles H. *Letters from the Saints: Early Renaissance and Reformation Periods from St. Thomas Aquinas to Bl. Robert Southwell.* New York: Philosophical Library, 1958. 214 pp. Includes bibliography.

Includes letters to the following saints: Bridget of Sweden, Catherine of Siena, Joan of Arc, Teresa of Avila, Catherine of Ricci, Anne of Jesus, and Jane Lestonnac.

Wright, Elliott. *Holy Company: Christian Heroes and Heroines.* New York: Macmillan, 1980. 272 pp. Good documentation, bibliography.

Brief accounts of 70 men and women who mirrored Christ's teachings in their living. The individuals are varied: lay, clergy, ancient, medieval, modern, several nationalities and ethnic backgrounds, different theologies, and from Eastern and Western Christianity.

Wyker, Mossie. *Church Women in the Scheme of Things*. St. Louis: Bethany Press, 1953. 117 pp. No documentation, bibliography, or index.
Examines the role of Protestant women in their churches. Includes policy-making levels and ordination.

## Early Christianity

Augustine. *Confessions*. Translated by Edward Bouverie Pusey. Chicago: Encyclopaedia Britannica, 1955.
See esp. books 6 and 13.

Borresen, Kari Elisabeth. *Subordination and Equivalence: The Nature and Role of Woman in Augustine and Thomas Aquinas*. Washington DC: University Press of America, 1981. 369 pp. Excellent bibliography, index of biblical references, index of persons, index of Latin terms, and index of references to Augustine in Aquinas.
A systematic exposition of the teachings of Augustine and Aquinas on the nature of woman and her role.

Brittain, Alfred. *Woman in All Ages and in All Countries: Women of Early Christianity*. New York: Gordon Press. 1976. Reprint of 1907 edition. 390 pp. No bibliography, no index.
Discusses lives of several women from the first century to the Byzantine era.

Brittain, Alfred and Mitchell Carroll. *Women of Early Christianity*. Woman in All Ages and in All Countries series. New York: Gordon Press, 1976. 390 pp. No documentation, bibliography, or index.
Examines women during persecution, the time of Constantine, post-Nicene mothers, nuns of the primitive church, women in the Roman and Frankish church, and individual women of influence.

Castelli, Elizabeth. "Virginity and Its Meaning for Women's Sexuality in Early Christianity." *Journal of Feminist Studies in Religion* 15 (Spring 1986): 61-88. Well documented.

Chadwick, H., ed. *Alexandrian Christianity.* Library of Christian Classics. Philadelphia: Westminster Press, 1954.
    See esp. "On Marriage" by Clement of Alexandria, 40-92.

Chrysotom, John. *On Virginity; Against Marriage.* Studies in Women and Religion 9. Translation by Sally R. Shore; introduction by Elizabeth A. Clark. New York: Edwin Mellen Press, 1983. 157 pp. Includes bibliographic references.

Clark, Elizabeth A. *Ascetic Piety and Women's Faith: Essays on Late Ancient Christianity.* Studies in Women and Religion 20. Lewiston NY: Edwin Mellen Press, 1986. 427 pp. Index.
    Thirteen essays on women in general and on individual women.

_____. "Ascetic Renunciation and Feminine Advancement: A Paradox of Late Ancient Christianity." *Anglican Theological Review* 63 (July 1981): 240-57.
    Argues that the church offered women more freedom and power in asceticism than in marriage.

_____. *Jerome, Chrysotom, and Friends: Essays and Translations.* Studies in Women and Religion 1. New York: Edwin Mellen Press, 1979. 254 pp.
    Contrasts the Fathers' negative writings on women with their friendships with women. Demonstrates the elevated status of celibate women but not married women.

_____. "John Chrysotom and the Subintroductae." *Church History* 46 (June 1977): 171-85. Good documentation.
    On spiritual marriages.

_____. *The Life of Melania the Younger.* Studies in Women and Religion 14. New York: Edwin Mellen Press, 1984. 299 pp. Excellent notes, extensive bibliography, index.

Clark introduces the writing with a detailed introduction of the questions regarding the language of the original text. She translates the complete text, then provides extensive commentary on it.

_____. "Sexual Politics in the Writings of John Chrysostom." *Anglican Theological Review* 59 (January 1975): 3-19.
Examines Chrysostom's use of celibacy and its influence in patriarchal practices.

_____. *Women in the Early Church. Message of the Fathers of the Church.* Vol. 13. Wilmington DE: Michael Glazier, 1983. 260 pp. Includes bibliography.
Fine overview of the Fathers' attitude toward women in patristic literature. Writings of the Fathers are arranged by topics.

Cristiani, Leon. *The Story of Monica and Her Son Augustine.* Boston: Daughters of St. Paul, 1977. 170 pp.
Material on Monica (Monnica, 331/2–387) is scant so this undocumented information may be useful.

Danielou, Jean. *The Ministry of Women in the Early Church.* New York: Morehouse-Barlow, 1961. 31 pp.
Uses writings of early church fathers to examine the role of women in early Christianity.

Davies, Stevan L. *The Revolt of the Widows: The Social World of the Apocryphal Acts.* Carbondale: Southern Illinois University Press, 1980. 139 pp. Includes bibliography and index.
See esp. "Women in the Apocryphal Acts" and "Widows and the Apocryphal Acts."

Donaldson, James. *Woman: Her Position and Influence in Ancient Greece and Rome, and among the Early Christians.* London and New York: Longmans, Green, and Co. 1907. 278 pp. Includes bibliography and index.
Discussion of early Christianity is minimal.

Eckenstein, Lina. *The Women of Early Christianity.* London: The Faith Press, 1935. 159 pp. Documented, no bibliography, includes index.

Part 4 (97-153) deals with women after the New Testament period: women in Rome, prophets, martyrs, and heretics.

Egeria. *Egeria: Diary of a Pilgrimage.* Ancient Christian Writers series 38. New York: Newman Press, 1970. 287 pp. Repr.: in *A Lost Tradition: Women Writers of the Early Church,* by Wilson-Kastner et al. Washington DC: University Press of America, 1981. Includes bibliographic references.

Ephrem the Syrian. *The Harp of the Spirit.* Translated by Sebastian Brock. San Bernardino CA: Borgo Press, 1984. Includes bibliography.
See esp. "Hymns on Virginity" and "Hymns on Mary."

Glover, Terrot Reaveley. *Life and Letters in the Fourth Century.* New York: Russell and Russell, 1968.
"Women Pilgrims" (125-47) describes the life of fourth-century Christian pilgrims. Documented.

Gregory of Nyssa. *The Life of St. Macrina.* Translated by W. K. Lowther Clarke. Early Church Classics. London: SPCK, 1916. 79 pp.

Gryson, Roger. *The Ministry of Women in the Early Church.* Translated by Jean Laporte and Mary Louise Hall. Collegeville MN: Liturgical Press, 1976. 156 pp. Includes bibliography.
Examines Greek and Latin writers of the first to sixth centuries.

Heine, Susanne. *Women and Early Christianity: Are the Feminist Scholars Right?.* London: SCM, 1987. 182 pp. Includes bibliographic references, indexes.
Counters the presuppositions and methods of early feminist interpretations of church history.

Hennecke, Edgar, Wilhelm Schneemelcher, R. McL. Wilson, eds. *New Testament Apocrypha.* Vol. 1, *Gospels and Related Writings.* Philadelphia: Westminster Press, 1963.
See "Gospels under the Names of Holy Women" (338-44).

Hickey, Anne E. *Women of the Roman Aristocracy as Christian Monastics.* Studies in Religion 1. Ann Arbor MI: UMI Research Press. 1987. 151 pp. Thorough documentation, bibliography, index.
A historical-sociological study of female asceticism focusing on the women associated with Jerome and Rufinus.

Irvin, Dorothy. "The Ministry of Women in the Early Church." *Duke Divinity School Review* (Spring 1980): 76-86. Well documented, bibliography.

Jerome. *Selected Letters of St. Jerome.* Translated by F. A. Wright. Loeb Classical Library London: William Heinemann, 1933. 510 pp. Significant writings on women.

King, Karen L., ed., *Images of the Feminine in Gnosticism.* Studies in Antiquity and Christianity series. Philadelphia: Fortress Press, 1988. 455 pp. Includes bibliography, index.
Collection of essays and responses.

Klawiter, Frederick C. "The Role of Martyrdom and Persecution in Developing the Priestly Authority of Women in Early Christianity: A Case Study of Montanism." *Christian History* 49 (September 1980): 251-61. Good documentation.

Laporte, Jean. *The Role of Women in Early Christianity.* Studies in Women and Religion series 7. New York: Edwin Mellen Press, 1982. 189 pp. Excellent bibliography, four indexes.
Excellent resource. Collection of primary materials with introductions. Topics include martyrdom, conjugal life, contemplative life, ministry, and woman as symbol.

Lightman, Marjorie, and William Zeisel. "Univira: An Example of Continuity and Change in Roman Society." *Christian History* 46 (March 1977): 19-32. Good documentation.
On Christian women who married only once.

McKenna, Sister Mary Lawrence. *Women of the Church: Role and Renewal.* New York: P. J. Kennedy, 1967. 192 pp. Documented, index.

A study of the ecclesial orders of widows, virgins, and deaconesses in the early church, their interconnections, and influence on later orders.

McNabb, Vincent. "Was the Rule of St. Augustine Written for Melania the Younger?" *Journal of Theological Studies* 20 (1919).
Intriguing question thoroughly addressed.

McNamara, Jo Ann. *A New Song: Celibate Women in the First Three Centuries.* New York: Harrington Park Press, 1983. 154 pp. Well documented, good bibliography, index.
Argues that the celibate life was not forced on women but that they chose it.

_____. "Sexuality Equality and the Cult of Virginity in Early Christian Thought." *Feminist Studies* 3 (1976): 145-58.

_____. "Wives and Widows in Early Christian Thought." *International Journal of Women's Studies* (November/December 1979): 575-92. Well documented.

Menzies, Allan, ed. *The Ante-Nicene Fathers: Translations of the Writings of the Fathers down to A.D. 325.* Vol. 10. Edinburgh: T. & T. Clark; Grand Rapids MI: William B. Eerdmans, various editions and reprints.
See "The Acts of Xanthippe and Polyxena" (203-17).

Oulton, John Ernest Leonard. *Alexandrian Christianity.* Library of Christian Classics 2. Philadelphia: Westminister Press, 1954. 475 pp. Includes bibliographical footnotes.
See esp. "On Marriage" (40-92).

Palladius. *Palladius: the Lausiac History.* Ancient Christian Writers series. Westminster MD: Newman Press, 1965. 265 pp.
Includes several writings regarding women. Also see "women" in the index.

Roberts, Alexander, James Donaldson, et al., eds. *The Ante-Nicene Fathers: Translations of the Writings of the Fathers Down to A.D. 325.* Ten

volumes. Edinburgh: T. & T. Clark; Grand Rapids MI: Wm. B. Eerd-
mans, various editions and reprints (most recent is 1993); orig. 1885ff.
Includes numerous valuable documents reflecting attitudes of
Fathers toward women and the church.

Ruether, Rosemary Radford, ed. *Religion and Sexism: Images of Woman in
the Jewish and Christian Traditions*. New York: Simon & Schuster,
1974. 356 pp. A few suggested readings; index.
See esp. "Misogynism and Virginal Feminism in the Fathers of the
Church" by Ruether (150-83).

Ryrie, Charles Caldwell. *The Role of Women in the Church*. Chicago: Moody
Press, 1970. 155 pp. Documentation, two indexes.
Examines the status of 2nd- and 3rd-century women in the life of
the church.

Schaff Philip, ed. *A Select Library of the Nicene and Post-Nicene Fathers of the
Christian Church*. First series. 14 vols. Repr.: Grand Rapids: William B.
Eerdmans, 1974. Index.

Scholer, David M., ed. *Women in Early Christianity*. Studies in Early Christianity 14. New York: Garland Publishing, 1993. 339 pp. Documentation.
Essays examine theology, individuals, roles, and writing of the
Fathers.

Thurston, Bonnie Bowman. *The Widows: A Women's Ministry in the Early
Church*. Minneapolis: Fortress Press, 1989. 141 pp. Good bibliography.
Some discussion of writings of Clement, Ignatius, Polycarp, and
Tertullian.

Torjesen, Karen J. *When Women Were Priests: Women's Leadership in the
Early Church and the Scandal of Their Subordination in the Rise of
Christiantiy*. San Francisco: Harper & Row, 1993. 278 pp. Document-
ed, index.
Traces the decline of women's leadership in the church and the
reasons for that decline. Shows sharp contrast between the teaching and

practices of Jesus and the teachings and practices of developing Christianity.

Wiesen, David. *St. Jerome as a Satirist: A Study in Christian Latin Thought and Letters.* Ithaca NY: Cornell University Press, 1964. 290 pp. Good bibliography, index.

    See his letters and works on "Women and Marriage," 113-65.

Wilson-Kastner, Patricia, G. Ronald Kastner, Ann Millin, Rosemary Rader, and Jeremiah Reedy. *A Lost Tradition: Women Writers of the Early Church.* Washington DC: University Press of America, 1981. 180 pp. Fine bibliography.

    Four documents written by women in the early years of Christianity: Perpetua, Proba, Egeria, Eudokia. Excellent resource.

"Women in the Early Church." *Christian History* 7/1 (1988).

    Entire issue is devoted to the topic. See esp. the following: "The Neglected History of Women in the Early Church" by Catherine Kroeger (6-9); "Early Church Women and Heresy" by Ruth A. Tucker and Walter Liefield (9-11); "Early Church Heroines: Rulers, Prophets, and Martyrs" by Aida Besancon Spencer (12-19); and "The Early Controversies over Female Leadership" by Karen Torjesen (20-24).

Yarbrough, Anne. "Christianization in the Fourth Century: The Example of Roman Women." *Christian History* (June 1976): 149-65. Well documented.

## Medieval Period

Abelard and Heloise. *The Letters of Abelard and Heloise.* Trans. and intro. by Betty Radice. New York: Scholar's Press, 1986.

Abelard and Heloise. *The Letters of Abelard and Heloise.* Harmondsworth: Penquin Press, 1978. 309 pp. Maps, bibliography, index.

Anderson, Bonnie S. and Judith P. Zinsser. *A History of Their Own: Women in Europe from Prehistory to the Present.* Vol. 1. New York: Harper & Row, 1988.

See "'The Extraordinary' Joan of Arc and witchcraft persecutions" (151-73), and "The Patterns of Power and Limitation: The Tenth to the Seventeenth Centuries" (181-82).

Aquinas, Thomas. *Basic Writings of Saint Thomas Aquinas.* 2 vols. Edited and annotated by Anton C. Pegis. New York: Random House, 1945. See esp. question 92: "The Production of Woman."

_____. *Summa Theologiae.* New York: McGraw-Hill, 1964, 1966, 1968. Includes introductions, notes, appendixes, and glossaries. See esp. questions 92, 93, 98.

Atkinson, Clarissa W. *Mystic and Pilgrim: The "Book" and the World of Margery Kempe.* Ithaca NY: Cornell University Press, 1983. 241 pp. Fine bibliography; index.
    Examines Kempe's life in different contexts and proposes several ways of interpreting her life and autobiography.

Baker, Derek, ed. *Medieval Women.* Oxford: Basil Blackwell, 1978. 399 pp. Includes bibliographic references.
    Chapters on saints, nuns, and orders.

Barstow, Anne Llewellyn. *Joan of Arc: Heretic, Mystic, Shaman.* Studies in Women and Religion 17. Lewiston/Queenston NY: Edwin Mellen Press, 1986. 163 pp. Includes bibliography, index.
    Not a biography, but an examination of Joan of Arc's experience with religion.

Beer, Frances. *Women and Mystical Experience in the Middle Ages.* Woodbridge, Suffolk UK and Rochester NY: Boydell Press, 1992. 174 pp. Includes bibliography and index.
    Examines the texts and the social and historical contexts of Hildegard, Mechthild, and Julian. Beer draws some contrasts with the writings of two medieval men writing for women.

Bell, Rudolph M. *Holy Anorexia.* Chicago: University of Chicago Press, 1985. 248 pp. Extensive notes and bibliography; index.

Examines the lives of 170 holy women recognized by the Roman Catholic Church as especially religious and who lived in Italy between 1200 and the present and about whom there is sufficient information to study. More than half displayed characteristics of anorexia. Bell attempts to persuade the reader that the anorexia-like behavior of these holy women was a response to the patriarchal social structures in which they were confined.

Borresen, Kari Elisabeth. *See above*, Historical Periods: Early Christianity.

Boulding, Elise. *The Underside of History: A View of Women through Time.* Boulder CO: Westview Press, 1976.
    See "Women Religious in the Middle Ages" (453-72), a concise history of women's religious orders.

Bowie, Fiona, and Oliver Davies, eds. *Beguine Spirituality: Mystical Writings of Mechthild of Magdeburg, Beatrice of Nazareth, and Hadewijch of Brabant.* New York: Crossroad, 1990. 130 pp. Good bibliographical references.

Bradford, Clare M. "Julian of Norwich and Margaret Kempe." *Theology Today* 35 (July 1978): 153-58. Minimal documentation.

Braswell, Laura. "Saint Edburga of Winchester: A Study of Her Cult, A.D. 950–1500, with an Edition of the Fourteenth-Century Middle English and Latin *Lives.*" *Medieval Studies* 33 (1971): 292-333.
    Well documented.

Brunn, Emilie Zum, and Georgette Epiney-Burgard. *Women Mystics in Medieval Europe.* New York: Paragon House, 1989. 231 pp. Fine documentation, good bibliography, index.
    Provides introductions to and excerpts from Hildegard of Bingen, Mechthild of Magdeburg, Beatrice of Nazareth, Hadewijch of Antwerp, and Marguerite Porete.

Bynum, Caroline Walker. *Jesus as Mother: Studies in the Spirituality of the High Middle Ages.* Berkeley: University of California Press, 1982. 279 pp. Includes bibliography, index.

Examines women mystics of the 13th century and their contributions to the understanding of an androgynous God by focusing on his feminine nature.

Cardman, Francine. "The Medieval Question of Women and Orders." *The Thomist* 42 (October 1978): 582-99.
Traces the development of the question of women and orders in Peter Lombard's *Sentences* in the 12th century and relates it to advances in canon law regarding ordination of women.

Catherine of Siena. *The Dialogue.* Translation and introduction by Suzanne Noffke. Classics in Western Spirituality series. New York: Paulist Press, 1980. 398 pp. Includes selected bibliography, two indexes.
Format: questions or petitions to God with responses and explanations.

Catherine of Siena. *The Prayers of Catherine of Siena.* New York: Paulist Press, 1983. 257 pp. Includes bibliography, indexes.

Catherine of Siena. *Saint Catherine of Siena: as Seen in Her Letters.* Translated, edited, and introduced by Vida D. Scudder. New York: E. P. Dutton, 1911.
Includes "Brief Outline of Contemporary Public Events" and "Chief Events in the Life of Saint Catherine." A sizable and useful collection of letters.

Cholmeley, Katharine. *Margery Kempe: Genius and Mystic.* New York: Longmans, Green and Co. 1947. 118 pp.
Short, easily read, but undocumented biography.

Clissold, Stephen. *St. Teresa of Avila.* New York: Seabury Press, 1982. 272 pp. Concise notes, index.

Collins, Louise. *Memoirs of a Medieval Woman: The Life and Times of Margery Kempe.* New York: Harper & Row, 1983. Short bibliography.

Delany, Sheila. *A Legend of Holy Women: A Translation of Osbern Boken-ham's Legends of Holy Women*. Notre Dame IN: University of Notre Dame Press. 1992.

Bokenham, a 15th-century Englishman, wrote biographies or memorials to be read on the anniversary of the person's death. Includes 11 women.

Dronke, Peter. *Women Writers of the Middle Ages: A Critical Study of Texts from Perpetua (d. 203) to Marguerite Porete (d. 1310)*. Cambridge: Cambridge University Press, 1984. 338 pp. Good documentation. Includes bibliography, indexes.

Examines writings of Heloise, Hildegard of Bingen. Includes 33 pages of Hildegard's text in Latin.

Eckenstein, Lina. *Women under Monasticism*. New York: Russell and Russell, 1963. 496 pp. Index.

A comprehensive examination of institutions, functions, and contributions of women.

Elkins, Sharon. *See below*, Ethnic-National: British.

Francis and Clare. *Francis and Clare: The Complete Works*. Translation and introduction by Regis J. Armstrong and Ignatius C. Brady. Classics in Western Spirituality series. New York: Paulist Press, 1982. 256 pp. Includes bibliography, indexes.

Includes nine of Clare's writings.

Gies, Frances. *Joan of Arc: The Legend and the Reality*. New York: Harper & Row, 1959. 306 pp. Well documented, bibliography, index.

Gies, Frances and Joseph. *Women in the Middle Ages*. New York: Thomas Y. Crowell, 1978. 264 pp. Good bibliography, index.

See "Eve and Mary" for medieval church's conflicting concept of woman. Also see "An Abbess: Hildegarde of Bingen."

Giordani, Igino. *Saint Catherine of Siena: Doctor of the Church*. Trans. Thomas J. Tobin. Boston: Daughters of St. Paul, 1975. 258 pp. Some documentation.

Goodich, Michael. "The Contours of Female Piety in Later Medieval Hagiography." *Christian History* 50 (March 1981): 20-32. Good documentation.

Guyon, Jeanne. *Sweet Smelling Myrrh: The Autobiography of Madame Guyon.* Trans. Thomas Allen. New Caanan CT: Keats, 1980. 192 pp.

Guyon, Jeanne. *Union with God: Including 22 of Madame Guyon's Poems.* Library of Spiritual Classics. Augusta ME: Christian Books, 1981. 117 pp.

Hadewijch, Beguine. *Hadewijch, the Complete Works.* Classics in Western Spirituality series. New York: Paulist Press, 1980. 412 pp. Includes bibliography, indexes.
Flemish 13th-century Beguines.

Hamilton, Elizabeth. *Heloise.* Garden City NY: Doubleday, 1967. 234 pp. Includes bibliography.

Healy, Emma Therese. *Women According to Saint Bonaventure.* Erie PA: Villa Maria College, 1956. 275 pp. Includes bibliography.
Thorough examination of the ideas of Saint Bonaventure of the 13th century as a "Champion of Christian Womanhood."

Heimmel, Jennifer P. *"God Is Our Mother": Julian of Norwich and the Medieval Image of Christian Feminine Divinity.* Salzburg: Institute für Anglistick und Amerikanistik, Universität Salzburg, 1982. 111 pp. Good bibliography.
Good discussion of Julian's contributions.

Hildegard of Bingen. *Hildegard of Bingen's Book of Divine Works with Letters and Songs.* Edited and introduced by Matthew Fox. Santa Fe NM: Bear and Co., 1987. 408 pp. Appendixes facilitate use of the text.

Hollis, Stephanie. *Anglo-Saxon Women and the Early Church: Sharing a Common Fate.* Rochester NY: Boydell Press. 1992. 323 pp. Thorough documentation, bibliography, index.

Literature by clerics regarding Anglo-Saxon women in the 8th and early 9th centuries in Europe. Fine examination of primary materials.

Holloway, Julia B., trans. *Saint Bride and Her Book: Bridget of Sweden's Revelations.* Newburyport MA: Focus Texts. 1992. 164 pp. Well documented, large bibliography, large index.
    Fourteenth-century saint. Historical introduction. Primary materials predominate.

Institoris, Henricus, ed. *Malleus Maleficarum* [by Jakob Sprenger with Henry Kramer, 1487. ET: *Witches' Hammer*]. Repr. London: Pushkin Press, 1948. 277 pp.
    A church document and the official handbook for inquistors of witches in the Middle Ages.

Juliana [also Julian] of Norwich. *Revelations of Divine Love.* Trans. with an intro. by M. L. del Mastro. Garden City NY: Doubleday, 1977. 240 pp. Short bibliography.
    The substantial introduction examines Juliana as a person, the essence of her message, and her mysticism. Primary devotional literature. Discussion of manuscript sources in the introduction.

Julian [also Juliana] of Norwich. *Showings.* Trans. and intro. by Edmund Colledge and James Walsh. New York: Paulist Press, 1978. 367 pp. Includes bibliography, extensive indexes.
    The sixteen revelations or visions of the 14th-century anchoress who addressed the feminine side of God, the humanity of Christ, and divine love.

King, Margaret L. "The Religious Retreat of Isotta Nogarola (1418–1466): Sexism and Its Consequences in the Fifteenth Century." *Signs* 3 (Summer 1978): 807-22. Well documented. Concludes with bibliographic essay.
    Examines the experience of 15th-century woman.

Kirshner, Julius, and Suzanne F. Wemple. *Women of the Medieval World: Essays in Honor of John H. Mundy.* London and New York: Basil Blackwell, 1987. 380 pp. Index.

Includes "Teste David cum Sibylla: The Significance of the Sibylline Tradition in the Middle Ages" by Bernard McGinn (7-35); "A Legacy of Miracles: Hagiography and Nunneries in Merovingian Gaul" by Jo Ann McNamara (36-53); "Bishops as Marital Advisors in the Ninth Century" by Jane Bishop (54-84); "S. Salvatore / S. Giulia: A Case Study in the Endowment and Patronage of a Major Female Monastery in Northern Italy" by Suzanne F. Wemple (85-102); "Stephen Langton's 'Sermo de Virginibus'" by Phyllis B. Roberts (103-18); "'Ancilla Dei': The Servant as Saint in the Late Middle Ages" by Michael Goodich (119-36); "Prostitution and Repentance in Late Medieval Perpigan" by Leah Lydia Otis (137-60); and "Female Imagery: A Clue to the Role of Joachim's Order of Fiore" by Stephen Wesley (161-78).

Klapisch-Zuber, Christiane, ed. *A History of Women in the West.* Vol. 2. *Silences of the Middle Ages.* Cambridge MA: Harvard University Press, 1992.
    See "The Clerical Gaze," by Jacques Dalarun, 15-42, for a discussion of the contradictory messages of the church to women.

Kors, Alan Charles, and Edward Peters, eds. *Witchcraft in Europe, 1100–1700. A Documentary History.* Philadelphia: University of Pennsylvania Press, 1972. 382 pp. Includes bibliographic references.
    Excellent collection of documents.

Labarge, Margaret Wade. *A Small Sound of the Trumpet: Women in Medieval Life.* Boston: Beacon Press, 1986. 271 pp. Well documented, suggested readings.
    Especially note "The Mould for Medieval Women"; the section on theories, laws and teachings: "Women Who Prayed: Nuns and Beguines"; and "Women Who Prayed: Recluses and Mystics."

Leclercq, Jean. *Women and Saint Bernard of Clairvaux.* Trans. Marie-Bernard Said OSB. Kalamazoo MI: Cistercian Publications, 1989. 175 pp. Documented, no bibliography, no index.
    Examines Bernard's texts, letters to women, relationship to nuns and queens, his concepts of masculine and feminine, his relationship to misogynists, and the myths about Saint Bernard.

Lucas, Angela M. *Women in the Middle Ages: Religion, Marriage, and Letters.* New York: St. Martin's Press, 1988. 214 pp. Fine bibliography, index. Part 1, "Women and Religion," 3-58, includes early Christian writings, the Church Fathers' concern with virginity, monastic communities, and nuns and their tensions with the church hierachy over the changing roles of nuns.

McDonnell, Ernest W. *The Beguines and Beghards in Medieval Culture, with Special Emphasis on the Belgian Scene.* New Brunswick NJ: Rutgers University Press, 1954. 643 pp. Extensive bibliography, extensive index. Thorough, well-documented discussion.

Mauriac, Francois. *Saint Margaret of Cortona.* New York: Philosophical Library, 1948. 231 pp.
Regarding the 13th-century saint.

Morris, Joan. *The Lady Was a Bishop: The Hidden History of Women with Clerical Ordination and the Jurisdiction of Bishops.* New York: Macmillan, 1973. 192 pp. Well documented, good bibliography, index.
A careful account of women who had the jurisdiction of bishops or overseers, focusing on the quasiepiscopal abbesses in eight European countries.

Nichols, John A., and Lillian Thomas Shank. *Medieval Religious Women.* Vol. 1. Kalamazoo MI: Cistercian Publications, 1984. 299 pp. Fine documentation, index.
Fourteen essays examine the experience of religious medieval women from several perspectives.

Peers, E. Allison. *Mother of Carmel: A Portrait of St. Teresa of Jesus.* London: SCM Press, 1946. 163 pp.

Peroud, Regine. *Joan of Arc by Herself and Her Witnesses.* New York: Stein and Day, 1966. 287 pp. No documentation; index.

Petroff, Elizabeth Alvilda, ed. *Medieval Women's Visionary Literature.* New York: Oxford University Press, 1986. 402 pp. Outstanding bibliography; index.

Primary selections. Excellent resource for exploring writings of medieval women.

Pisan, Christine de. *The Book of the City of Ladies.* New York: Persea Books, 1982. 281 pp.
Stories of heroines of the past mingled with commentary on society's attitudes toward women.

Power, Eileen. *Medieval English Nunneries c. 1275–1535.* New York: Biblo and Tannen, 1964. 724 pp. Bibliography.
Thorough treatment of subjects such as the nunneries' structure, daily life, property, education, enclosure, morals, and reform.

Rahner, Hugo. *Saint Ignatius Loyola: Letters to Women.* Edinburgh: Nelson, 1960. 565 pp. Well documented, index.
Correspondence with "Royal Ladies," "Noble Ladies," "Benefactresses," "Spiritual Daughters," "Mothers of Fellow Jesuits," and women friends.

Ruether, Rosemary Radford. "The Persecution of Witches: A Case of Sexism and Agism?" *Christianity and Crisis* 34 (23 December 1974): 291-95.

Russell, Jeffrey Burton. *Witchcraft in the Middle Ages.* London: Cornell University Press, 1972. 394 pp. Good documentation.
Discusses medieval witchcraft in relation to medieval society, Catharism, antinomianism, scholasticism, and the Inquisition.

Sackville-West, Victoria. *Saint Joan of Arc.* New York: Literary Guild, 1936. 395 pp. Several useful appendixes.

Sackville-West, Victoria. *The Eagle and the Dove, A Study in Contrasts: St. Teresa of Avila, St. Therese of Lisieux.* Garden City NY: Doubleday, Doran, and Co., 1944. 175 pp.

Scott, Walter Sidney. *Jeanne d' Arc.* London: Harrap, 1974. 239 pp. Extensive and very useful appendixes including a large annotated bibliography.

Shahar, Shulamith. *The Fourth Estate: A History of Women in the Middle Ages.* New York: Methuen, 1983. 351 pp. Well documented, bibliographic references, index.
   See esp. the chapters on nuns (22-64) and on witches and the heretical movements (251-80).

Taylor, Henry Osborn. *The Medieval Mind: A History of the Development of Thought and Emotion in the Middle Ages.* 2 vols. Cambridge MA: Harvard University Press, 1949.
   In vol. 1, see "Mystic Visions of Ascetic Women" (458-86), focusing on Elizabeth of Schonau, Hildegard of Bingen, Mary of Ognies, Liutgard of Tongern, and Mechthild of Magdeburg. Documented. In vol. 2, see "The Heart of Heloise" with strong use of primary materials (29-54).

Teresa of Avila. *The Collected Works of St. Teresa of Avila.* Vol 1. Washington DC: Institute of Carmelite Studies Publications, 1976. 406 pp. Includes explanatory notes, index of biblical references, and large subject index.
   Contains "The Book of Her Life," "Spiritual Testimonies," and her "Soliloquies."

_____. *Interior Castle.* Trans. and ed. by E. Allison Peers. Garden City NY: Image Books, 1961. 235 pp.
   Spiritual insights of a noted saint.

_____. *The Life of Teresa of Jesus: The Autobiography of St. Teresa of Avila.* Trans. E. Allison Peers. Garden City NY: Doubleday, 1960. 399 pp. Explanatory notes. (Also trans. David Lewis [Westminster MD: Newman Press, 1951] 526 pp. Index.)
   Includes an outline of Teresa's life.

_____. *The Way of Perfection.* New York: Doubleday, 1964. 280 pp.
   Advises spiritual perfection through prayer.

Thornton, Martin. *Margery Kempe: An Example in the English Pastoral Tradition.* London: SPCK, 1960. 120 pp.

Commentary on *The Book of Margery Kempe* and her type of spirituality. Includes a "Classified Skeletal Commentary." A useful aid to reading and understanding *The Book of Margery Kempe.*

Warner, Marina. *Joan of Arc: The Image of Female Heroism.* New York: Alfred A. Knopf, 1981. 349 pp. Thoroughly documented, includes bibliographic references, index.

Wemple, Suzanne Fonay. *Women in Frankish Society: Marriage and the Cloister, 500 to 900.* Philadelphia: University of Pennsylvania Press, 1981. 348 pp. Thoroughly documented, extensive bibliography, index.
    Part 2, "Women in Religious Life" (127-88), addresses life in the church, monasticism, asceticism, and religious communities.

Williams, Charles. *See above,* Historical Periods: General History.

Wilson, Katarina M., ed. *Medieval Women Writers.* Athens: University of Georgia Press, 1984. 366 pp. Well documented. Includes bibliographies.
    Introduces each writer before providing excerpts from her writings. Includes Hildegard of Bingen, Mechthild of Magdelburg, Hadewijch, Marguerite Porete, Saint Bridget, Saint Catherine of Siena, Julian of Norwich, Margery Kempe.

"Women in the Medieval Church." *Christian History* 10:2 (1991). Entire issue devoted to the topic.

## Reformation Period

Alexander, J. H. *Ladies of the Reformation: Short Biographies of Distinguished Ladies of the Sixteenth Century.* Harpenden, England: Gospel Standard Strict Baptist Trust, 1978.
    Includes discussions of Jeanne d' Albrecht, Anna Reinhard (Zwingli's wife), Katherine von Bora (Luther's wife), Idelette de Bure (Calvin's wife), Marjorie Bowes (Knox's wife), three martyrs from the Netherlands, and various royal women.

Anderson, Bonnie S., and Judith P. Zinsser. *A History of Their Own: Women in Europe from Prehistory to the Present.* Vol. 1. New York: Harper & Row, 1988.

In vol. 1, see "Authority Given and Taken Away: The Protestant and Catholic Reformation" (228-52) and "The Legacy of the Protestant Reformation" (264-66).

Bainton, Roland D. *Women of the Reformation in France and England.* Boston: Beacon Press, 1975. 287 pp. Includes bibliography, index.
   Biographical sketches of royalty and commoners, relating each to the context of her era.

_____. *Women of the Reformation in Germany and Italy.* Minneapolis: Augsburg Publishing House, 1971. 279 pp. Includes table, maps, bibliography.
   Well-documented accounts of fifteen individuals plus a chapter on "Women of the Anabaptists."

_____. *Women of the Reformation: From Spain to Scandinavia.* Minneapolis: Augsburg Publishing House, 1977. 240 pp. Documentation, index.
   Discussions of 28 women from Spain, Portugal, Scotland, England, Denmark, Norway, Poland, Sweden, Hungary, and Transylvania.

Barton, F. Whitfield. *Calvin and the Duchess.* Louisville: Westminster-John Knox Press, 1989. 247 pp. Sound documentation using primary sources. Includes bibliography, no index.
   Examines the correspondence of John Calvin and Renee of France, a duchess sympathetic to Protestantism.

Blaisdell, Charmarie J. "Calvin's Letters to Women: The Courting of Ladies in High Places." *Sixteenth Century Journal* 13 (Fall 1982): 67-84.

Boulding, Elise. *The Underside of History: A View of Women through Time.* Boulder CO: Westview Press, 1976.
   See esp. "Religious Women of the Reformation and the Counter-Reformation" (546-51). An examination of women at various strata of society.

Chrisman, Miriam V. "Women of the Reformation in Strasburg, 1490–1530." *Archive for Reformation History* 63 (1972): 143-68.

Dallmann, William. *Kate Luther*. Milwaukee: Northwestern Publishing House, 1941. 123 pp.
Includes a good selection of photos, sketches, and art prints.

Douglas, Jane Dempsey. "Christian Freedom: What Calvin Learned at the School of Women." *Christian History* 53 (June 1984): 155-73. Good documentation.

————. *Women, Freedom, and Calvin*. Philadelphia: Westminister Press, 1985. 155 pp. Includes bibliography, index.
Examines Calvin's views of women through an examination of this theology.

Greaves, Richard L., ed. *Triumph Over Silence: Women in Protestant History*. Westport CT: Greenwood Press, 1985. 295 pp. Includes bibliography, index.
Five essays dealing with Luther, Calvin, Anabaptists, and English nonconformity; women's experience in New England is also addressed.

Harkness, Georgia Elam. *John Calvin: The Man and His Ethics*. New York: Henry Holt, 1931. 266 pp. Includes bibiliographic references.

Irwin, Joyce L. *Woman in Radical Protestantism 1525–1675*. Studies in Women and Religion series: 1800–1930. New York: Edwin Mellen Press, 1979. 258 pp. Includes bibliography, index.
Writings and sermons from the Protestant era. Includes the subjects of women in the church and women as preachers and prophets. Writers are both well known and little known.

Karant-Nunn, Susan C. "Continuity and Change: Some Effects of the Reformation on the Women of Zwickau." *Sixteenth Century Journal* 13 (Fall 1982): 67-84.
Zwickau was the largest city in the territory of Frederick the Wise. The last section discusses the religious impact on women that diminished under Lutheranism.

Luther, Martin. "Table Talk." In *Luther's Works*, vol. 54, ed. Helut T. Lehmann. Philadelphia: Fortress Press, 1967.

A collection of the sayings of Luther including "Of Marriage and Celibacy." Includes several references to his wife Katherine.

————. *What Luther Says.* Vol. 3. Compiled by Ewald M. Plass. St. Louis: Concordia Publishing House, 1959.
Sayings on "Woman," 1456-60.

Petersen, William J. *Martin Luther Had a Wife.* Wheaton: Tyndale House, 1983. 160 pp. Undocumented. Brief bibliography.
Short discussions of the marriages of Martin and Katie Luther, John and Molly Wesley, Jonathan and Sarah Edwards, Dwight and Emma Moody, and William and Catherine Booth.

Roelker, Nancy L. "The Appeal of Calvinism to French Noblewomen of the Sixteenth Century," *Journal of Interdisciplinary History* 2 (Spring 1972): 391-418.
Examines the response of French noblewomen to Calvinism and provides hypotheses regarding why they responded as they did.

Roelker, Nancy L. "The Role of Noblewomen in the French Reformation." *Archive for Reformation History* 63 (November 1972): 168-95.

Ruether, Rosemary Radford, ed. *Religion and Sexism: Images of Woman in the Jewish and Christian Traditions.* New York: Simon & Schuster, 1974. 356 pp. A few suggested readings, index.
See esp. "Women and the Continental Reformation" (292-318) by Jane D. Douglas.

Siggins, Ian. *Luther and His Mother.* Philadelphia: Fortress Press, 1981. 96 pp. Well documented, good index.
Examines primary material, deals with controversies surrounding Hanna Luder, and the influence of her family on Martin.

Williams, Charles. *See above,* Historical Periods: General History.

Wyntjes, Sherrin Marshall. "Women in the Reformation Era." In *Becoming Visible: Women in European History,* ed. Renate Bridenthal, Claudia Koonz, and Susan M. Stuard, 165-91. Boston: Houghton Mifflin, 1987.

A concise history, well documented with suggested readings.

## Europe: Modern Period

Beevers, John. *Storm of Glory: The Story of St. Therese of Lisieux.* Garden City NJ: Doubleday, 1949. 196 pp.
One of the few biographies of Therese of Lisieux.

Brotherton, Anne. *See below,* Denominations: Catholic.

Hufton, Owen and Frank Tallett. "Communities of Women. The Religious Life and Public Service in Eighteenth-Century France." In *Connecting Spheres: Women in the Western World, 1500 to the Present,* ed. Marilyn J. Boxer and Jean H. Quataert, 75-85. New York: Oxford University Press, 1987.
Discussion of the changing role of religious communities and their contributions to society.

Phayer, Michael. *Protestant and Catholic Women in Nazi Germany.* Detroit: Wayne State University Press, 1990. 286 pp. Well documented, bibliography, index.
An examination of how Protestant and Catholic women experienced the Third Reich very differently.

Rapley, Elizabeth. *The Devotees: Women and Church in Seventeenth-Century France.* Studies in the History of Religion. Buffalo NY: McGill-Queens University Press, 1990. 283 pp. Well documented, bibliography, index.

Sharma, Arvind, and Katherine K. Young, eds. *Annual Review of Women in World Religions.* Vol. 11. *Heroic Women.* Albany NY: State University of New York Press, 1992. 168 pp.
Includes "Florence Nightingale: A Study in Heroic Altrusim," by Sheila McDonough.

ten Boom, Corrie, with Jamie Buckingham. *Tramp for the Lord.* Old Tappan NJ: Fleming H. Revell, 1974. 192 pp.

Therese of Lisieux. *General Correspondence.* Translated by John Clarke. Washington DC: Institute of Carmelite Studies, 1982. 687 pp.

Letters from Therese's childhood to the novitiate, including some facsimilies.

————. *St. Therese of Lisieux, Her Last Conversations.* Translated by John Clarke. Washington DC: Institute of Carmelite Studies, 1977. 332 pp. Chronological biographic guide, index.

————. *The Story of a Soul.* Westminster MD: Newman Press, 1954. 159 pp.
Story of Therese's spiritual journey.

## America: General History

Alexander, Jon, O.P. *American Personal Religious Accounts, 1600–1980: Toward an Inner History of America's Faiths.* Studies in American Religion 8. Lewiston NY: Edwin Mellen Press. 1983. 501 pp. Includes extensive annotated bibliography and index.
    Includes personal religious accounts of Anne Hutchinson, Anne Bradstreet, Sarah Osborn, Catherine Hummer, Ann Lee, Jemima Wilkinson, St. Elizabeth Seton, Ann Judson, Sojourner Truth, Elizabeth Cady Stanton, Phoebe Palmer, Ellen G. White, Amanda B. Smith, Frances Willard, Julia Ward Howe, Hannah W. Smith, Mary Baker Eddy, Emma Goldman, Jane Addams, Georgia Harkness, Carrie A. Nation, Alice Kruger, Aimee S. McPherson, Irma Lindheim, Dorothy Day, Mary McLeod Bethune, Robin Morgan, Annie Dillard, and Elisabeth Kubler-Ross.

Bailey, Janice. *Those Meddling Women.* Valley Forge PA: Judson Press. 1977. 95 pp. Documented, no bibliography, no index.
    Includes brief accounts of Anne Hutchinson and Sojourner Truth.

Beaver, R. Pierce. *American Protestant Women in World Mission.* Grand Rapids: Wm. B. Eerdmans, 1980. 237 pp. Documentation, bibliography, three indexes.
    Chronicles the involvement in and impact of Protestant women in foreign mission work. Both religious and social impact is addressed.

Boyer, Paul S. *Women in American Religion.* Philadelphia: University of Pennsylvania Press, 1980. 274 pp. Includes bibliographic references.

Boylan, Anne M. "Women in Groups: An Analysis of Women's Benevolent Organizations in New York and Boston, 1797–1840." *Journal of American History* 3 (1984): 497-523.

Brereton, Virginia Lieson and Christa Ressmeyer Klein, "American Women in Ministry: A History of Protestant Beginning Points." In *Women in American Religion,* ed. Janet Wilson James, 171-90. Philadelphia: University of Pennsylvania Press, 1980.

Calkins, Gladys Gilkey. *Follow Those Women: Church Women in the Ecumenical Movement. (A History of the Development of United Work among Women of the Protestant churches in the United States).* New York: United Church Women, 1961. 108 pp. Little documentation.
    The story of how Protestant women moved from involvement in missions to being united across denominational lines, and eventually to become a part of the National Council of Churches of Christ in the U.S.A.

Carpenter, Joel E. "The Fundamentalist Leaven and the Rise of an Evangelical United Front." In *The Evangelical Tradition in America,* ed. Leonard I. Sweet, 257-88. Macon GA: Mercer University Press, 1984.

Cavert, Inez M. *Women in American Church Life.* New York: Friendship Press, 1949. 93 pp. Minimal documentation, three appendixes.
    Focuses on the reaction to the place of women in church life, women as volunteers in denominational work, and women in interdenominational agencies.

DeBerg, Betty A. *Ungodly Women: Gender and the First Wave of American Fundamentalism.* Minneapolis: Fortress Press, 1990. 165 pp. Annotated bibliography of primary sources, index.
    Reactions of fundamentalism to women in church and society.

Frakes, Margaret. "Women's Status in the Churches." *Christian Century* 70 (14 October 1953): 1164-66.
    Report on the ordination and participation of women in policymaking activities in the following denominations: A.M.E., A.M.E. Zion, American Baptist, Augustana Lutheran, Church of the Brethren, Con-

gregational, Christian, Disciples of Christ, Evangelical and Reformed, Evangelical United Brethren, Friends, Methodist, Presbyterian Church U.S., Presbyterian Church USA, Protestant Episcopal, Reformed Church in America, and United Lutheran.

George, Carol V. R., ed. *Remember the Ladies: New Perspectives on Women in American History.* Syracuse NY: Syracuse University Press, 1975. 201 pp. Includes bibliographic references and index.
    See "Anne Hutchinson and the Revolution Which Never Happened," a well-documented account of her trials and their significance.

Hewitt, Nancy A. "The Perimeters of Women's Power in American Religion." In *The Evangelical Tradition in America,* ed. Leonard I. Sweet, 233-56. Macon, GA: Mercer University Press, 1984.

Hill, Patricia P. *The World Their Household: The American Women's Foreign Mission Movement and Cultural Transformation 1870–1920.* Ann Arbor MI: University of Michigan Press, 1985. 231 pp. Well documented, good bibliography, extensive index.

Hunter, Fannie McDowell. *Women Preachers.* Dallas: Berachah Printing Co., 1905. 100 pp. No documentation.
    A defense of women preachers that includes an autobiographical sketch. Autobiographical experiences of other women preachers also are included.

Hunter, Jane. *The Gospel of Gentility: American Women Missionaries in Turn-of-the-Century China.* New Haven CT: Yale University Press, 1984. 318 pp. Well documented, index.

James, Janet Wilson, ed. "Women and Religion," *American Quarterly* (Winter 1978). Entire issue devoted to this topic.

Lerner, Gerda, ed. *The Female Experience: An American Documentary.* The American Heritage series. Indianapolis: Bobbs-Merrill, 1977. 509 pp. Includes bibliography, index.

Ninety-one readings from the 17th to 20th centuries on a wide range of subjects. Includes "The Trial of a Heretic: Anne Hutchinson 1637" giving a brief background and then excerpts from her trials.

Scott, Anne Firor. *The Southern Lady: From Pedestal to Politics, 1830–1930.* Chicago: University of Chicago Press, 1970.
See "The Lord Helps Those . . . ," a brief survey of religious involvement (134-63). Documented. A more concise version of the same material is "Women, Religion, and Social Change in the South, 1830–1930," in *Religion and the Solid South*, ed. Samuel S. Hill, Jr. (Nashville: Abingdon Press, 1972).

Sinclair, Andrew. *The Better Half: The Emancipation of the American Woman.* New York: Harper & Row, 1965. 401 pp. Good notes.
See chapters on "The Feminist Bibles," "The Reverend Suffragists," "The Feminists against the Churches," and "The Heirs of Anne Hutchinson."

Smith-Rosenberg, Carroll. "Women and Religious Revivals: Antiritualism, Liminality, and the Emergence of the American Bourgeoisie." In *The Evangelical Tradition in America*, ed. Leonard I. Sweet, 199-31. Macon GA: Mercer University Press, 1984.

Stratton, Joanna L. *Pioneer Women: Voices from the Kansas Frontier.* New York: Simon & Schuster, 1981. 319 pp.
"The Frontier Church" describes women's role in Kansan churches, illustrated frequently with writings of frontier women.

Twing, Mary A.E. "Women's Work in the American Church." *Church Review* (January 1891): 182-92.

Tyler, Alice Felt. *Freedom's Ferment: Phases of American Social History to 1860.* Freeport NY: Books for Libraries Press, 1970.
These chapters integrate women into the historical accounts: "Evangelical Religion," " Transcendentalism," "Millenialism and Spiritualism," "Religious Communism in America," "The Shaker Communities," and "The Rights of Women."

## America: Colonial Period

Adams, C. F. *Three Episodes of Massachusetts History*. Volume 1. Boston: Houghton, Mifflin, and Co., 1896.
    Includes material on Anne Hutchinson and the Antinomian controversy (371-532).

Augur, Helen. *American Jezebel: The Life of Anne Hutchinson*. New York: Brentano's, 1930. 320 pp. Includes bibliography, index.

Battis, Emery. *Saints and Sectaries: Anne Hutchinson and the Antinomian Controversy in the Massachusetts Bay Colony*. Chapel Hill: University of North Carolina Press, 1962. 379 pp. Seven very useful appendixes, an extensive bibliography, and a good index.
    Examines and analyzes the controversy from a psychological perspective.

Bremer, Francis J. *Anne Hutchinson: Troubler of the Puritan Zion*. Huntington NY: Robert E. Krieger Publishing Co. 1981. 152 pp. Bibliographic essay.
    Fourteen essays centered around the topics of Anne Hutchinson, the religious dispute, the trial, the social dimension, and the sexual dimension.

Curtis, Edith. *Ann Hutchinson: A Biography*. Cambridge MA: Washburn and Thomas, 1930. 122 pp. Some documentation. Five appendixes of primary material.

Ellis, George E. *Puritan Age and Rule in the Colony of the Massachusetts Bay Colony, 1629–1685*. New York: Burt Franklin, 1970. Reprint of 1888 document. 576 pp. Index.
    Includes discussion of Anne Hutchinson and the Antinomian controversy (300-62).

Frey, Sylvia R., and Marian J. Morton. *New World, New Roles: A Documentary History of Women in Preindustrial America*. Contributions to Women's Studies 65. New York: Greenwood Press, 1986. 246 pp. Includes bibliography, index.

See "Women and Religion in the Seventeenth Century" (61-88) and "Women and Religion, 1700–1815" (181-201). Both articles incorporate primary materials.

George, Carol V. R. *See above*, Historical Periods: America: General History.

Greaves, Richard L. *See above*, Historical Periods: Reformation Period.

Green, Harry Clinton, and Mary Wolcott. *The Pioneer Mothers of America: A Record of the More Notable Women of the Early Days of the Country, and Partnership of the Colonial and Revolutionary Periods.* 2 vols. New York: G. P. Putnam's Sons, 1912.
  In vol. 1, material on Ann Hutchinson (201-38), but includes no documentataion and is of limited value. Vol. 2 is of no value on the subject of women in church history.

Hall, David D. *The Antinomian Controversy, 1636–1638: A Documentary History.* Durham NC: Duke University Press, 1990. 453 pp. Includes bibliographical references.
  See "The Examination of Mrs. Anne Hutchinson at the Court in Newton" (311-48); and "A Report of the Trial of Mrs. Anne Hutchinson Before the Church at Boston" (349-88).

Hansen, Chadwick. *Witchcraft at Salem.* New York: Braziller, 1969. 252 pp. Includes bibliographic references.
  A thorough examination.

Holliday, Carl. *Women's Life in Colonial Days.* Williamstown MA: Corner House Publishers, 1968. Reprint of 1922 edition. 319 pp. Documentation, suggested bibliography, and index.
  "Colonial Woman and Religion" (3-69) is a discussion of the effect of religion on women, involvement of women in religion, religious rebels, and witchcraft.

Hosmer, James Kendall, ed. *Winthrop's Journal: History of New England 1630–1649.* New York: Charles Scribner's Sons, 1908.

Hutchinson, Thomas. *The History of the Colony and Province of Massachusetts Bay.* Vol. 2. Cambridge: Harvard University Press, 1936.
    See "The Examination of Mrs. Anne Hutchinson at the Court at Newtown" (366-91), a transcription of proceedings of her trial.

King, Anne. "Anne Hutchinson and Anne Bradstreet: Literature and Experience, Faith and Works in the Massachusetts Bay Colony." *International Journal of Women's Studies* (September/October 1978): 445-67. Good documentation.

Koehler, Lyle. "The Case of the American Jezebel: Anne Hutchinson and Female Agitation during the Years of Antinomian Turmoil, 1636–1640. In *Women's America: Refocusing the Past,* by Linda K. Kerber and Jane Sherron De Hart. New York: Oxford University Press, 1991.

Lang, Amy Schrager. *Prophetic Woman: Anne Hutchinson and the Problem of Dissent in the Literature of New England.* Berkeley: University of California Press, 1987. 272 pp. Includes bibliography, index.
    Using Nathaniel Hawthorne's portrait of Hutchinson as a point of departure, Lang concludes that the problem of antinomianism and the problem of female empowerment were entwined all along. Shows how Emerson, Hawthorne, and Stowe deal with gender and dissent.

Leonard, Eugenie Andruss. *The Dear-Bought Heritage.* Philadelphia, University of Pennsylvania Press, 1965. 658 pp. Includes bibliography.
    "She Struggled with God and the Devil" (349-90) is a good survey of colonial women's experience with religion.

Lerner, Gerda. *See above,* Historical Periods: America: General History.

Malmsheimer, Lonna M. "Daughters of Zion: New England Roots of American Feminism." *New England Quarterly* 50 (September 1977): 484-504. Documented.
    The shift in attitudes toward women is traced in sermons.

Masson, Margaret W. "The Typology of the Female as a Model for the Regenerate: Puritan Preaching, 1690–1730." *Signs* 2 (Winter 1976): 304-15. Well documented.

Mather, Cotton. *On Witchcraft, Being the Wonders of the Invisible World.* Mt. Vernon NY: Peter Pauper Press, 1950. 172 pp.
Descriptions of witches, addresses on witchcraft, accounts of trials.

Mather, Cotton. *Ornaments for the Daughters of Zion: A Facsimile Reproduction.* Delmar NY: Scholars' Facsimiles and Reprints, 1978. Reprint of 1741 edition. 116 pp.
Mather's assessment of the role and status of women in 17th-century America, including religious life. The editor's introduction examines some of Mather's works relating to women.

Moran, Gerald F. "'Sisters' in Christ: Women and the Church in Seventeenth-Century New England." In *Women in American Religion,* ed. Janet Wilson James, 47-65. Philadelphia: University of Pennsylvania Press, 1980.

Morgan, Edmund S. "The Case Against Anne Hutchinson." *New England Quarterly* 10 (December 1937): 635-49. Documented.

Nevins, Winfield S. *Witchcraft in Salem Village in 1692.* New York: Burt Franklin, 1971. Reprint of 1916 edition. 272 pp. Some documentation, photos, prints, and index.
Appendixes include a list of the accused and other primary documents.

Porterfield, Amanda. *Female Piety in Puritan New England.* Religion in America series. New York: Oxford University Press, 1992. 207 pp. Well documented, with bibliography and index.
Discussion of how men (Hooker, Shepard, and Mather) stressed female piety to excercise authority over women and how women (Hutchinson and Bradstreet) used female piety to gain authority for women.

Ruether, Rosemary Radford, and Rosemary Skinner Keller, eds. *Women and Religion in America.* 3 vols. San Francisco: Harper & Row, 1981, 1983, 1986. Well documented, thorough indexes.
Vol. 2, *The Colonial and Revolutionary Periods: A Documentary History,* includes the following: "American Indian Women and Religion"

by Petterson and Druke; "Women and Religion in Spanish America" by Asuncion Allen; "Women in Colonial French America" by Christine Allen; "New England Women: Ideology and Experience in First Generation Puritanism (1630–1650)" by Keller; "The Religious Experience of Southern Women" by Alice E. Mathews; "Black Women and Religion in the Colonial Period" by Lillian Ashcraft Webb; "Women in Sectarian and Utopian Groups" by Reuther and Prelinger; "Women and Revivalism: The Puritan and Wesleyan Traditions" by Blauvelt and Keller; and "Women, Civil Religion, and the American Revolution" by Keller.

Topics are introduced with some background before the documents are presented. A very useful resource.

Rugg, Winnifred King. *Unafraid: A Life of Anne Hutchinson.* Boston: Houghton Mifflin Co., 1930. 263 pp. Includes bibliography and index.

Starkey, Marion. *The Devil in Massachusetts: A Modern Inquiry into the Salem Witch Trials.* New York: Alfred A. Knoff, 1949. 314 pp. Includes bibliography, index.

Stein, Stephen J. "A Note on Anne Dutton, Eighteenth Century Evangelical." *Christian History* 44 (December 1975): 485-91. Good documentation.

Concise assessment of Dutton's influence.

Thompson, Roger. *See below,* Ethnic-National: British.

Ulrich, Laurel Thatcher. "Vertuous Women Found: New England Ministerial Literature, 1668–1735." In *Women in American Religion,* ed. Janet Wilson James, 67-87. Philadelphia: University of Pennsylvania Press, 1980.

A portrait of model spiritual women of the time.

Voth, Anne. *Women in the New Eden.* Washington DC: University Press of America, 1983. Documentation, bibliography.

See "Margaret Wintrop: Puritan Wife" (33-70). Voth describes the Puritan ideal for woman, and shows through Winthrop's letter how she tried to meet the ideal.

Williams, Selma R. *Divine Rebel: The Life of Anne Marbury Hutchinson.* New York: Holt, Rinehart, and Winston, 1981. 246 pp. Good documentation, good bibliography, index.

Winthrop, John. *Wintrop's Journal: History of New England, 1630–1649.* 2 vols. Edited by James K. Hosmer. New York: Scribner's Sons, 1908. Volume 1 contains several entries regarding Anne Hutchinson.

## America: Nineteenth Century

Anthony, Susan B. *Elizabeth Cady Stanton / Susan B. Anthony: Correspondence, Writings, Speeches.* Edited with a critical commentary by Ellen Carol DuBois. New York: Schocken Books, 1981.

Barnes, Gilbert H., and Dwight L. Dumond, eds. *Letters of Theodore Dwight Weld, Angelina Grimke Weld and Sarah Grimke, 1822–1844,* 2 vols. New York: D. Appleton-Century, 1934.

Bednarowski, Mary Farrell. "Outside the Mainstream: Women's Religion and Women Religious Leaders in Nineteenth Century America." *Journal of the American Academy of Religion* 48 (June 1980): 207-31.
  Examines the doctrine of and role of women in Shakerism, Spiritualism, Christian Science, and Theosophy. Fine documentation.

Birney, Catherine H. *See below,* Social Reform.

Boylan, Anne M. "Evangelical Womanhood in the Nineteenth Century: The Role of Women in Sunday Schools." *Feminist Studies* 4 (1978): 62-80. Well documented.

Brereton, Virginia Lieson. *From Sin to Salvation: Stories of Women's Conversions, 1800 to the Present.* Bloomington IN: Indiana Univeristy Press. 1991. 152 pp. Well documented, fine bibliography, index.
  Fine examination of the patterns, language, and meaning of women's conversion stories noting women's initiative as well as their dependence on God.

Brumberg, Joan Jacobs. "Zenanas and Girlless Villages: The Ethnology of American Evangelical Women, 1870–1910." *Journal of American History* (1982): 347-71. Well documented.
Insightful examination of influence of evangelical women in shaping America's definition of self.

Cott, Nancy F. "Young Women in the Second Great Awakening in New England." *Feminist Studies* 3 (1975): 15-29. Extensive notes.

Douglas, Ann. *The Feminization of American Culture*. New York: Alfred A. Knopf, 1977. 403 pp. Includes bibliographic references, index.
Argues that 19th-century middle-class women and liberal Protestant clergy formed an alliance to shape culture. Appendixes identify 30 women, some of note, and 30 ministers, several of note.

Epstein, Barbara L. *The Politics of Domesticity: Women, Evangelism and Temperance in Nineteenth Century America*. Middleton CT: Wesleyan University Press, 1981. 188 pp. Documented, good bibliography, index.
Interesting discussions of the religious conversions of 18th- and 19th-century women and of the work of the Women's Christian Temperance Union.

Friedman, Jean E. *The Enclosed Garden: Women and Community in the Evangelical South, 1830–1900*. Chapel Hill: University of North Carolina Press, 1985. 180 pp. Well documented, valuable bibliography, index.
Extensive discussion of the influences of the church on women.

Gage, Matilda Joslyn. "Woman, Church, and State." In *The History of Woman Suffrage 1848–1861*, 3 vols, by Elizabeth Cady Stanton, Susan B. Anthony, and Matilda Joslyn Gage, 1:753-99. New York: Arno Press, 1969.

Gage, Matilda Joslyn. *Women, Church and State, the Original Expose of Male Collaboration Against the Female Sex*. Watertown MA: Persephone Press, 1980. Reprint of 1893 original. 554 pp.
Examines influences of government and religion on women. Daring for its time (and for ours!).

Garber, Rebecca Perryman. "The Social Gospel and Its View of Women and
the Women's Movement, 1880–1918." Master's thesis, Trinity
Evangelical Divinity School (Deerfield IL), 1978. 147 pp. Thorough
bibliography.
    Examines Washington Gladden's and Walter Rauschenbusch's view
of women and the women's movement, focusing finally on their
reactions to woman's role in the church. Concludes that both men were
influenced by the "cult of motherhood" and therefore tended to
accomodate rather than advocate women's issues of the time. Appendix
2 is Rauschenbusch's manuscript notes entitled "The Woman Problem."

Gifford, Carolyn de Swarte, ed. *The Nineteenth Century American Methodist
Itinerant Preacher's Wife*. Women in American Protestant Religion
Series: 1800–1930. New York: Garland Publishing, 1987. 160 pp.
    Two 19th-century writings describe the life of the preacher's wife.

Gilchrist, Beth Bradford. *The Life of Mary Lyon*. Boston: Houghton Mifflin,
1910. 462 pp. Includes bibliography.
    Mary Lyon was the founder of Mount Holyoke College.

Green, Elizabeth Alden. *Mary Lyon and Mount Holyoke: Opening the Gates*.
Hanover NH: University Press of New England, 1979. 406 pp. Fine
notes, bibliography, extensive index.
    Biography of Mary Lyon, a pioneer in colleges for women. Includes
accounts of the involvement of several women in Mount Holyoke
Female Seminary's early years.

Grimke, Angelina Emily. *Letters to Catherine E. Beecher*. The Black Heritage
Library Collection. Freeport NY: Books for Libraries Press, 1971. 130
pp.
    Includes Grimke's letters on abolition.

Grimke, Angelina and Sarah. *The Public Years of Sarah and Angelina
Grimke: Selected Writings, 1835–1839*. New York: Columbia University
Press, 1989. 380 pp. Includes bibliography, index.
    Eight major documents. Includes Angelina's "Appeal to the
Christian Women of the South" and Sarah's "An Epistle to the Clergy
of the Southern States."

Grimshaw, Patricia. *Paths of Duty: American Missionary Wives in Nineteenth-Century Hawaii.* Honolulu: University of Hawaii Press. 1989. 246 pp. Well documented, good bibliography, index.

Recovers the stories of mission wives and their influential role in educating national girls and women both spiritually and culturally. Also details wives' struggle with their own roles.

Hanaford, Phebe A. *Women of the Century.* Boston: B. B. Russell, 1877. 648 pp.

Includes chapters on women preachers, women missionaries, women educators, and "women of faith." Discusses individuals as well as the general topic.

Hardesty, Nancy A. *Women Called to Witness: Evangelical Feminism in the 19th Century.* Nashville: Abingdon Press, 1984. 176 pp. Includes bibliographic references, index.

Traces the roots of American feminism from women's early missions and charity organizations in the early 1800s through evangelical revivalism to the passage of the Nineteenth Amendment in 1920. The appendix is a chronological listing of "defenses of woman's ministry" from 1808 to 1930.

Hardesty, Nancy A. *Your Daughters Shall Prophesy: Revivalism and Feminism in the Age of Finney.* Chicago Studies in the History of American Religion 5. Brooklyn: Carlson Publishing, 1991. 192 pp. Well documented, bibliography, index.

Argues that Charles Finney's revivals had a major positive impact on Christian women, raising them to a position of equality. The appendix is a bibliographic listing of "Defenses of Women's Ministry" from 1808 to 1976; most are 19th-century documents.

Harkness, Georgia Elam. "Pioneer Women in Ministry." *Religion in Life* 39 (Summer 1970): 261-71. Documented.

Focuses on the 19th century.

Hassey, Jannette. *See above,* Historical Periods: General History.

Holley, Marietta. *See below,* Denominations: Methodist.

Hyatt, Irwin T., Jr. *Our Ordered Lives Confess: Three Nineteenth-Century American Missionaries in East Shantung.* Cambridge MA: Harvard University Press, 1976.
  One part is a concise account of a woman, Charlotte (Lottie) Diggs Moon, pp. 65-136.

Jacobs, Harriet A. *See below,* Ethnic-National: African American.

James, Janet Wilson, ed. *Women in American Religion.* Philadelphia: University of Pennsylvania Press, 1980. 271 pp. Documented.
  Thirteen essays on a wide range of topics.

Jeffrey, Julie Roy. *Frontier Women: The Transmississippi West, 1840–1880.* New York: Hill and Wang, 1979. 240 pp. Large bibliography, index.
  Describes the ways women were involved in religion (95-105); for other scattered passages, see "religion" in index.

Kimball, Gayle. *The Religious Ideas of Harriet Beecher Stowe: Her Gospel of Womanhood.* Studies in Women and Religion 8. Lewiston NY: Edwin Mellen Press, 1982. 206 pp. Excellent bibliography on Stowe and her interpreters.
  Portrays woman as a central agent of salvation, a theme of Stowe's works.

Krueger, Christine L. *The Readers' Repentance: Women Preachers, Women Writers, and Nineteenth-Century Social Discourse.* Chicago: University of Chicago Press, 1992. 350 pp. Well documented, bibliography, index.
  Methodist preachers and writers including Hannah More, Charlotte Elizabeth Tonna, Elizabeth Gaskell, and George Eliot.

Lasser, Carol, and Marlene Merrill, eds. *Soul Mates: The Oberlin Correspondence of Lucy Stone and Antoinette Brown, 1846–1850.* Oberlin OH: Oberlin College, 1983. 100 pp. Biographical notes included.
  Reveals dreams and struggles of two noted women.

Loewenberg, Bert James, and Ruth Bogin. *See below,* Ethnic-National: African-American.

Lutz, Alma. *Emma Willard: Pioneer Educator of American Women.* Boston: Beacon Press, 1964. 143 pp. Undocumented; index.

McDannell, Colleen. *The Christian Home in Victorian America, 1840–1900.* Bloomington IN: Indiana University Press, 1986. 193 pp. Includes bibliography, index.
    Includes an examination of women's contribution to Christianity domestically.

Majors, Monroe. *See below,* Ethnic-National: African-American.

Marshall, Helen E. *See below,* Social Reform.

Mott, Lucretia. *See below,* Denominations: Quakers.

Parker, Gail, ed. *Oven Birds: American Women on Womanhood, 1820–1920.* Garden City NY: Doubleday, 1972. 387 pp. Includes bibliographic references.
    Includes Catherine Beecher's "An Address to the Christian Women of America" and Angelina Grimke Weld's "Appeal to the Christian Women of the South."

Phelps, Elizabeth Stuart. "A Woman's Pulpit." *Atlantic Monthly* 26 (July 1870): 11-22.
    First-person account of a woman's struggle to become a licensed minister and serve as a minister in the 19th century.

Prentiss, George L. *The Life and Letters of Elizabeth Prentiss.* New York: Edward O. Jenkins, 1882. 573 pp.
    Uses autobiographical materials to record the life of a devout woman who was a pastor's wife and writer in the 19th century.

Ruether, Rosemary Radford, and Rosemary Skinner Keller, eds. *Women and Religion in America.* 3 vols. San Francisco: Harper & Row, 1981, 1983, 1986. Well documented, thorough indexes.
    Vol. 1, *The Nineteenth Century: A Documentary History,* includes the following: "Women and Revivalism" by Marth T. Blauvelt; "Women in Utopian Movements" by Reuther; "The Leadership of Nuns in

Immigran Catholicism" by Mary Ewens, O.P.; "The Jewish Woman's Encounter with American Culture" by Ann Braude; "The Struggle for the Right to Preach" by Barbara B. Zikmund; "Lay Women in the Protestant Tradition" by Keller; and "Women in Social Reform Movements" by Carolyn Gifford.

Topics are introduced with some background before the documents are presented. A very useful resource.

Ryan, Mary P. "A Women's Awakening: Evangelical Religion and the Families of Utica, N.Y., 1800–1840." In *Women in American Religion*, ed. Janet Wilson James, 89-110. Philadelphia: University of Pennsylvania Press, 1980.

Sleeper, Sarah. *Memoir of the Late Martha Hazeltine Smith*. Women in American Protestant Religion Series: 1800–1930. New York: Garland Publishing, 1987. Reprint of 1843 document. 294 pp.
Smith was a teacher at New Hampton Female Seminary.

Stanton, Elizabeth. *Eighty Years and More (1815–1897 Reminiscences of Elizabeth Cady Stanton)*. New York: European Publishing Co., 1898. 474 pp. Includes bibliographic references, index.
See chapter on "Woman and Theology" and the last chapter for her account of "The Woman's Bible."

Stanton, Elizabeth Cady. *The Woman's Bible*. 2 vols. Women: Images and Realities series. New York: Arno Press, 1972.
Commentaries on selected books of the Bible.

Stone, Lucy. *Friends and Sisters: Letters between Lucy Stone and Antoinette Brown Blackwell, 1846–1893*. Edited by Carol Lasser and Marlene Merrill. Urbana: University of Illinois Press, 1987. 278 pp. Includes bibliography, index.
Correspondence begins with their days at Oberlin College and reflects Stone's disapproval of Brown's choice of ministry as a career.

Sweet, Leonard I. *The Minister's Wife: Her Role in Nineteenth Century American Evangelicalism*. Philadelphia: Temple University Press, 1983. 327 pp. Excellent documentation, index.

Focus is on the 19th century, but also includes a thorough exploration of the influence of minister's wives in the development of women's ministry. From Katherine Luther's and Idelette Calvin's early patterns, to wives who served faithfully in the background, to female preachers, Sweet traces the emerging role of women in American religion.

Thoburn, J. M. *See below*, Denominations: Methodist.

Tucker, Ruth A. *See above*, Historical Periods: General History.

Vail, Albert L. *Mary Webb and the Mother Society.* Philadelphia: American Baptist Publication Society, 1914. 110 pp. No documentation.
    An account of the founding of the first woman's missionary society in 1800.

Welter, Barbara. "The Feminization of Religion in Nineteenth-Century America." In *Clio's Consciousness Raised: New Perspectives on the History of Women*, ed. Mary S. Hartman and Lois W. Banner, 137-57. New York: Harper & Row, 1974. Well documented.

Welter, Barbara. "She Hath Done What She Could: Protestant Women's Missionary Careers in Nineteenth-Century America." In *Women in American Religion*, ed. Janet Wilson James, 111-25. Philadelphia: University of Pennsylvania Press, 1980.

Wittenmyer, Annie. *Women's Work for Jesus.* Women in American Protestant Religion Series: 1800–1930. New York, Garland Publshing, 1987. Reprint of 1873 document. 240 pp.
    A charge to 19th-century women to become involved in virtually every area of church and society. Wittenmyer speaks boldly.

## America: Twentieth Century

Armstrong, Christopher. *Evelyn Underhill: An Introduction to Her Life and Writings.* Grand Rapids: William B. Eerdmans, 1976. 303 pp. Includes bibliography.
    Solid introduction to Underhill.

Balmer, Randall. "American Fundamentalism: The Ideal of Femininity." In *Fundamentalism and Gender*, ed. John S. Hawley, 47-62. New York: Oxford Univeristy Press, 1994. Well documented.

Boyer, Paul. "Minister's Wife, Widow, Reluctant Feminist: Catherine Marshall in the 1950s." in *Women in American Religion*, ed. Janet Wilson James, 251-71. Philadelphia: University of Pennsylvania Press, 1980.

Brown, Karen McCarthy. "Fundamentalism and the Control of Women." In *Fundamentalism and Gender*, ed. John S. Hawley, 175-201. New York: Oxford University Press, 1994. Well documented.

Buckingham, Jamie. *Daughter of Destiny: Kathryn Kuhlman, Her Story.* Plainfield NJ: Logos International, 1976. No documention, no bibliography.

Frakes, Margaret. "Theology Is Her Province." *Christian Century* 69 (24 September 1952): 1088-91.
   On Georgia Harkness.

Gifford, Carolyn de Swarte, ed. *The American Deaconess Movement in the Early Twentieth Century.* Woman in American Protestant Religion Series: 1800–1930. New York: Garland Publishing, 1987.
   The focus is on the Methodist Episcopal Church. See esp. "The Burden of the City" by Isabelle Horton. "The Early History of Deaconess Work and Training Schools for Women in American Methodism, 1883–1885" by the Woman's Home Missionary Society documents primarily women church professionals and the social gospel movement.

Graebner, Alan. "Birth Control and the Lutherans: The Missouri Synod as a Case Study." In *Women in American Religion*, ed. Janet Wilson James, 229-52. Philadelphia: University of Pennsylvania Press, 1980.

Harkness, Georgia Elma. *Christian Ethics.* New York: Abingdon Press, 1957. 240 pp.

Foundations of Christian ethics and implications for selected social issues.

_____. *Conflict in Religious Thought.* New York: Henry Holt and Co., 1929. 326 pp.

_____. *The Resources of Religion.* New York: Henry Holt and Co., 1936. 218 pp. Indexes.

_____. "A Spiritual Pilgrimage." *Christian Century* 56 (15 March 1939): 348-51. How My Mind Has Changed in This Decade series.

_____. *Understanding the Christian Faith.* New York: Abingdon-Cokesbury Press, 1947. 187 pp.
"Basic Christian convictions for the lay, not the lame, mind" (Harkness).

Hosier, Helen Kooiman. *Kathryn Kuhlman: The Life She Led, the Legacy She Left.* Old Tappan NJ: Fleming H. Revell, 1971. 160 pp. Scant documentation, no bibliography, no index.

Kuhlman, Katherine. *I Believe in Miracles.* Old Tappan NJ: Fleming H. Revell Co., 1975. 223 pp.

McPherson, Aimee Semple. *In the Service of the King: The Story of My Life.* New York: Boni and Liveright, 1927. 316 pp.

_____. *The Personal Testimony of Aimee Semple McPherson.* Los Angeles: Starling Press, 1984. 50 pp.

_____. *This is That: Personal Experiences, Sermons, and Writings of Aimee Semple McPherson.* Los Angeles: Echo Park Evangelistic Assoc., 1923. 791 pp.

Parker, Gail, ed. *See above,* Historical Periods: America: Nineteenth Century.

Rice, John R. *Bobbed Hair, Bossy Wives, and Women Preachers.* Wheaton IL: Sword of the Lord Publishers, 1941. 91 pp.

Addresses "three controversial subjects: (1) Is it a sin for women to cut their hair? (2) Must a wife be subject to, obedient to her husband, ruled by him? (3) Does God ever call or consent for women to be preachers, pastors, or evangelists?" Insists there is no controversy regarding what the Bible says of these matters.

Ruether, Rosemary Radford. *Faith and Fratricide: The Theological Roots of Anti-Semitism*. New York: Seabury Press, 1974. 294 pp.

_____. *Liberation Theology: Human Hope Confronts Christian History and American Power*. New York: Paulist Press, 1972. 194 pp. Bibliographic references.

_____, and Rosemary Skinner Keller, eds. *Women and Religion in America*. 3 vols. San Francisco: Harper & Row, 1981, 1983, 1986. Well documented, thorough indexes.
    Vol. 3, *1900–1968: A Documentary History*, includes the following: "Radical Victorians: The Quest for an Alternative Culture" by Reuther; "American Indian Women and Religion on the Southern Plains" by Kay Parker; "Something Within: Social Change and Collective Endurance in the Sacred World of Black Christian Women" by Dodson and Gilkes; "Women Struggle for an American Catholic Idenity" by Lorine M. Getz; "Women in Evangelical, Holiness, and Pentecostal Traditions" by Scanzoni and Setta; "Patterns of Laywomen's Leadership in Twentieth-Century Protestantism" by Keller; "Women in Religious Education: Pioneers for Women in Professional Ministry" by Dorothy J. Furnish; and "Winning Ordination for Women in Mainstream Protestant Churches" by Barbara B. Zirmund.
    Topics are introduced with some background before the documents are presented. A very useful resource.

Sayers, Dorothy Leigh. *Creed or Chaos? and Other Essays in Popular Theology*. London: Methuen, 1947. 88 pp.

_____. *The Mind of the Maker*. New York: Harcourt, Brace and Co. 1941.
    Commentary on selected Christian concepts.

Scudder, Vida Dutton. *On Journey.* New York: E. P. Dutton. 1937. 445 pp. Index.

_____. *The Privilege of Age: Essays Secular and Spiritual.* London: Dent and Co., 1939. 319 pp.

_____. *Socialism and Character.* Boston: Houghton Mifflin, 1912. 430 pp. See the chapter "The Apologia of Religion."

Steele, Robert V. P. *Storming Heaven: The Lives and Turmoils of Minnie Kennedy and Aimee Semple McPherson.* New York: William Morrow and Co., 1970. 364 pp. Includes photos and bibliographic references. Biography of Aimee and her mother.

Tucker, Ruth A. *See above,* Historical Periods: General History.

Underhill, Evelyn. *Collected Papers of Evelyn Underhill.* New York: Longmans, Green, 1946. 240 pp. Includes a list of Underhill's writings, 37-38.

_____. *The Letters of Evelyn Underhill.* New York: Longmans, Green, 1943. 344 pp.

_____. *Mixed Pasture: Twelve Essays and Addresses.* Freeport NY: Books for Libraries Press, 1968. Reprint of 1933 edition. 233 pp.

Utley, Uldine. *Why I Am a Preacher.* Women in American Protestant Religion Series: 1800–1930. New York: Garland Press, 1987. Reprint of 1931 edition. 152 pp. An account of preaching at Madison Square Garden in 1926. Includes four sermons.

# Ethnic and/or National Groups
(*see also* America and Europe under Historical Periods)

## Africa

Isham, Mary. *See below*, Denominations: Methodist.

Jacob, Sylvia. *See below*, Ethnic-National: African-American.

Oduyoye, Mercy A., and Musimbi R. Kanyaro, eds. *The Will to Arise: Women, Tradition, and the Church in Africa.* Maryknoll NY: Orbis Books, 1992. 230 pp. Some documentation, no bibliography, no index.
   Collection of thirteen essays by women African theologians on the relationship of African culture, sexual practices, and Christianity.

Webster, John C. B., and Ellen Low. *See above*, Historical Periods: General History.

## African-American

Acornley, John H. *The Colored Lady Evangelist: Being the Life, Labors and Experiences of Mrs. Harriet A. Baker.* Women in American Protestant Religion Series, 1800–1930. New York: Garland Publishing, 1987. Reprint of 1892 document.
   Includes a short biography and some of her sermons.

Andrews, William L., ed. *Sisters of the Spirit: Three Black Women's Autobiographies of the Nineteeth Century.* Bloomington: Indiana University Press, 1986. 245 pp. Well documented.
   Autobiographies of three African-American women Methodist preachers: Jarena Lee, Zilpha Elaw, and Julia A. J. Foote. Introduction provides background on each woman.

Bambara, Toni Cade, ed. *The Black Woman: An Anthology.* New York: New ✓ American Library, 1970. 256 pp.
   See "The Diary of an African Nun," by Alice Walker, 38-41.

Bradford, Sarah Elizabeth. *Harriet Tubman, the Moses of Her People.* Seacaucus NJ: Citadel Press, 1980. Reprint of 1886 edition. 149 pp. No documentation. Appendix includes letters to Tubman.

Conrad, Earl. *Harriet Tubman.* New York: Paul S. Erikson, 1969. 248 pp. Good documentation.

Day, Helen Caldwell. *Color, Ebony.* New York: Sheed and Ward, 1951. 182 pp. No documentation, bibliography, or index.
    African-American Methodist who became an active Catholic volunteer worker.

Fauset, Arthur Huff. *Sojourner Truth: God's Faithful Pilgrim.* New York: Russell and Russell, 1971. Reprint of 1938 edition. 187 pp. Includes bibliography, index.

Harley, Sharon, and Rosalyn Terborg-Penn, eds. *The African-American Woman: Struggles and Images.* Port Washington NY: Kennikat Press, 1978.
    See "Nannie Burroughs and the Education of Black Women" by Evelyn Brooks Barnett, 97-108.

Haviland, Laura. *A Woman's Lifework: Labors and Experiences.* Miami: Mnemosyne Publishing Co., 1969. 554 pp.
    A personal account of a woman involved in several types of home mission work during the 19th century.

Hedgeman, Anna Arnold. *The Gift of Chaos: Decades of American Discontent.* New York: Oxford University Press, 1977. 249 pp. Includes bibliographic references and index.
    Note "Religion and Justice" as seen by an African-American.

Higginbotham, Evelyn Brooks. *Righteous Discontent: The Women's Movement in the Black Baptist Church 1880–1920.* Cambridge MA: Harvard University Press, 1993. 306 pp. Excellent documentation and index.
    Focuses primarily on women in the National Baptist Convention and their significant role the church, community, and society.

Holt, Rackham. *Mary McLeon Bethune: A Biography.* Garden City NY: Doubleday, 1964. 302 pp. Undocumented.
African-American Methodist educator, founder of Bethune-Cookman College.

Humez, Jean, ed. *Gifts of Power: The Writings of Rebecca Cox Jackson, Black Visionary and Shaker Eldress.* Amherst: University of Massachusetts Press, 1981. 368 pp. Textual notes, bibliographic essay, glossary of proper names.
Appendix includes writings of Rebecca Perot, "Documents: Female Preaching and the A. M. E. Church, 1820–1852," and "Documents: Shaker Doctrine."

Jacob, Sylvia, ed. *Black Americans and the Missionary Movement in Africa.* Contributions in African-American and African Studies 66. Westport CT: Greenwood Press, 1982. 255 pp. Includes bibliographic essay, index.
See "Their 'Special Mission': African-American Women as Missionaries to the Congo, 1894–1937" (155-75). Well documented.

Jacobs, Harriet A. *Incidents in the Life of a Slave Girl: Written by Herself.* Cambridge MA: Harvard University Press, 1987. 306 pp. Includes bibliography, index.
See "The Church and Slavery," 68-75.

Jackson, Rebecca. *Gifts of Power: The Writings of Rebecca Jackson, Black Visionary, Shaker Eldress.* Ed. Jean McMahon Humez. Amherst: University of Massachusetts Press, 1981. 368 pp. Fine annotated bibliography.
See esp. "Female Preaching and the A. M. E. Church, 1820–1852."

Johnson, Suzan D. *See above,* Historical Periods: General History.

Leffael, Dolores C. and Janet L. Sims. "Mary McLeod Bethune—The Educator; Also Including Selected Annotated Bibliography." *Journal of Negro Education* 45 (June 1976): 342-59. Fine bibliography.

Lerner, Gerda, ed. *Black Women in White America: A Documentary History.*
New York: Random House, 1973. 230 pp. Includes bibliography.
See section 2, "The Struggle for Education," esp. the chapter on
school founders; and section 7, "The Monster Prejudice," the chapter
on the YWCA.

Loewenberg, Bert James, and Ruth Bogin, eds. *Black Women in Nineteenth
Century American Life: Their Words, Their Thoughts, Their Feelings.*
University Park PA: Pennsylvania State University Press, 1976. 355 pp.
Excellent bibliography, index.
Autobiographical material from "Elizabeth," Jarena Lee, Amanda
Berry Smith, Sojourner Truth, and three women preachers.

McAfee, Sara J. *History of the Woman's Missionary Society in the Colored
Methodist Episcopal Church.* Phenix City AL: Phenix City Herald, 1945.
469 pp. No documentation.

Majors, Monroe A. *Noted Negro Women: Their Triumphs and Activities.*
Freeport NY: Books for Libraries Press, 1971. Reprint of 1893 edition.
365 pp. No documentation, some sketches.
Brief accounts of 311 African-American women in diverse roles.
Focuses on the 19th century.

Mitchell, Ella Pearson, ed. *Those Preachin' Women: Sermons by Black Women
Preachers.* Valley Forge PA: Judson Press, 1985. 126 pp.
Includes sermons by Laura Sinclair, Carolyn Ann Knight, Deborah
McGill-Jackson, Katie G. Cannon, Yvonne V. Delk, Nan M. Brown,
Mary Ann Bellinger, Sharon E. Williams, Marjorie Leeper Booker, Clara
Mills-Bradford, Beverly J. Shamana, Peggy R. Scott, Margrie Lewter-
Simmons, and Suzan D. Johnson.

Mitchell, Ella Pearson, ed. *Those Preaching Women: More Sermons by Black
Women Preachers.* Vol. 2. Valley Forge: Judson Press, 1988. 109 pp.
Fourteen sermons by contemporary ordained black women. Some
documentation.

Murray, Pauli. *Song in a Weary Throat: An American Pilgimage.* Knoxville:
University of Tennessee Press, 1989. 451 pp. Index.

Autobiography of an African-American activist and Episcopal priest.

Pauli, Hertha Ernestine. *Her Name Was Sojourner Truth.* New York: Avon Books, 1976. 250 pp. Includes bibliography and index.

Rogers, Cornish. "Blacks and the Feminists." *Christian Century* 91 (13 February 1974): 172-73.
Brief assessment of problems facing feminism in African-American churches.

Sasson, Diane. *See below,* Denominations: Shakers.

Scruggs, L. A. *Women of Distinction: Remarkable in Works and Invincible in Character.* Raleigh NC: L. A. Scruggs, 1892; Ann Arbor MI: University Microfilms International facsimile, 1983. 382 pp. No bibliography and no index.
Covers 88 women. Some general articles on Atlanta Univeristy, Fisk University, Hartshorn Memorial College, Scotia Seminary, and St. Augustine School.

Smith, Amanda. *An Autobiography: The Story of the Lord's Dealings with Mrs. Amanda Smith the Colored Evangelist.* New York: Oxford University Press, 1988. Repr.: Women in American Protestant Religion Series, 1880–1930. New York: Garland Publishing, 1988. 506 pp.
An account of a slave girl who become an effective evangelist in America, England, and India.

Tatum, Noreen Dunn. *See below,* Denominations: Methodists.

Wessinger, Catherine. *See above,* Historical Periods: General History.

Williams, Richard E. *See below,* Denominations: Shakers.

Young, Rosa. *Light in the Dark Belt: The Story of Rosa Young as Told by Herself.* St. Louis: Concordia Publishing House, 1929. 148 pp.
Autobiography of African-American woman who began Lutheran work in Alabama.

## Asian

Beck, James R. *See below*, Ethnic-National: British.

Boulding, Elise. *The Underside of History: A View of Women through Time.* Boulder CO: Westview Press, 1976.
"A Note on Religion and the Status of Women in India" (400-405); "Catholic Pioneers in Europe" (568-70).

Hardesty, Nancy A. *See above*, Historical Periods: General History.

Harrison, Ted. *Much Beloved Daughter: The Story of Florence Li Tim Oi.* Wilton CT: Morehouse-Barlow, 1985. 109 pp. No documentation. Includes bibliography, index.
Regarding a Chinese Anglican priest.

Isham, Mary. *See below*, Denominations: Methodist.

Kwok, Pui-lan. *Chinese Women and Christianity 1860–1927.* American Academy of Religion series 75. Edited by Susan Thistlethwaite. Atlanta: Scholars Press, 1992. 225 pp. Documented, extensive bibliography, no index.
Includes discussions of mission work among women, women's religious participation, leadership, and social reform activity.

Webster, John C. B., and Ellen Low. *See above*, Historical Periods: General History.

Wilson, Carol Green. *See below*, Denominations: Presbyterian.

## British

Anderson, James. *Memorable Women of the Puritan Times.* Volume 2. London: Blackie and Son, 1862. 408 pp. Documented, three appendixes include primary documents.
Especially note the discussions of Elizabeth Bunyan, wife of John Bunyan; Agnes Beaumont, friend of John Bunyan; Elizabeth Gaunt, wife of William Gaunt; and Lady Lisle.

Barbour, Hugh. *See below*, Denominations: Quaker.

Beck, James R. *Dorothy Carey: The Tragic and Untold Story of Mrs. William Carey.* Grand Rapids: Baker Book House, 1992. 254 pp. Well documented, includes bibliography, index.
A sympathetic biography of a much-maligned pioneer missionary wife about whom little of substance has been written.

Booth, Catherine Bramwell. *Catherine Booth: The Story of Her Loves.* London: Hodder and Stoughton, 1970. 467 pp. Documentation, index. Extensive use of Booth's letters.
Biography by her granddaughter.

Booth, Catherine (Munford). *Aggressive Christianity: Practical Sermons.* Boston: McDonald and Gill, 1883.

————. *Female Ministry: or, Woman's Right to Preach the Gospel.* New York: Salvation Army, 1975. Reprint of 1883 document.
A 15-page pamphlet Booth wrote in response to clergyman who opposed women preaching.

Booth-Tucker, F. de L. *The Life of Catherine Booth.* 2 vols. New York: Fleming H. Revell, 1893. Vol. 1, 663 pp.; vol. 2, 692 pp. including index.
Extensive material on Booth.

Brailsford, Mabel Richmond. *See below*, Denominations: Quaker.

Burder, Samuel. *Memoirs of Eminently Pious Women.* Philadephia: J. J. Woodward, 1834. 730 pp. Little documentation.
Accounts of 73 women, primarily English. The collection portrays religious experiences of women, both famous and little known. Gives the reader an exposure to the religious experience of a wide variety of women. May be difficult to obtain, but very useful.

Crawford, Patricia. *Women and Religion in England 1500–1720.* New York: Routledge, 1993. 268 pp. Thorough documentation, index.

Fine discussion of established churches, dissenting groups, and sects, esp. their teachings and practices that affected women.

Elkins, Sharon. *Holy Women of Twelfth-Century England.* Studies in Religion series. Chapel Hill: University of North Carolina Press. 1988. 244 pp. Well documented, fine bibliography, large index.
Examines the phenominal growth of female religious communities in the 12th century, collectively, regionally, and as specific orders.

Fell, Margaret. *See below,* Denominations: Quaker.

Fischer, Sandra K. "Elizabeth Cary and Tyranny, Domestic and Religious." In *Silent but for the Word: Tudor Women as Patrons, Translators, and Writers of Religious Works,* ed. Margaret P. Hanney, 225-37. Kent OH: Kent State University Press, 1985.

Greaves, Richard L. "The Role of Women in Early English Nonconformity." *Christian History* 52 (September 1983): 299-311. Good documentation. *See also* Greaves under Historical Periods: Reformation Period.

Hanney, Margaret P., ed. *Silent but for the Word: Tudor Women as Patrons, Translators, and Writers of Religious Works.* Kent, OH: Kent State University Press, 1985. 304 pp. Good bibliography, index.

Heeney, Brian. *The Women's Movement in the Church of England 1850–1930.* Oxford: Claredon Press, 1988. 144 pp. Includes bibliographic references, index.
Traces the history of the controversy over the role and status of women in the Church of England. See also a similar article by Heeney, "The Beginning of Church Feminism: Women and the Council of the Church of England 1897–1919," *Journal of Ecclesiastical History* 33 (January 1982): 89-109.

Johnson, Dale A. *Women in English Religion: 1700–1925.* Studies in Women and Religion 10. New York: Edwin Mellen Press, 1983. 353 pp. Good documentation, supplemental bibliography, index.
Recognizing that women's roles in the church during this period were scant, Johnson has collected documents that reflect the view of

women during these centuries. Documents reflect views of both women and men. Outstanding resource.

Knight, Helen C. compiler. *Lady Huntingdon and Her Friends.* Grand Rapids: Baker Book House, 1979. 292 pp.
    Quite a bit of material on Huntingdon, but no documentation.

Knowles, David, and R. Neville Hadcock. *Medieval Religious Houses, England and Wales.* London: Longmans, Green, 1953. 387 pp.
    See esp. the discussion of seven orders in "Houses of Nuns" (209-33).

Kunze,, Bonnelyn Young. *See below,* Denominations: Quaker.

Lehman, Edward C. *Women Clergy in England: Sexism, Modern Consciousness, and Church Viability.* Studies in Religion and Society series. Lewiston NY: Edwin Mellen Press, 1987. 210 pp. Includes bibliography and index.
    Some historical background included.

Lewalski, Barbara K. "Of God and Good Women: The Poems of Aemilia Lanyer." In *Silent but for the Word: Tudor Women as Patrons, Translators, and Writer of Religious Works,* ed. Margaret P. Hanney, 203-24. Kent OH: Kent State Univeristy Press, 1985.

McQuaid, Ina DeBord. *See below,* Denominations: Methodist.

Malmgreen, Gail, ed. *Religion in the Lives of English Women, 1760–1930.* London: Croom Helm, 1986. 295 pp. Well-documented anthology. Good index.
    Includes: "'Thine, Only Thine!' Women Hymn Writers in Britain, 1760–1835" by Margaret Maison (11-40); "Elisabeth Heyrick: Radical Quaker" by Kenneth Corfield (41-67); "Ann Carr and the Female Revivalists of Leeds" by D. Colin Dews (68-87); "Queen Victoria and Religion" by Walter L. Arnstein (88-128); "Virgin Vows: The Early Victorian Artists' Portrayal of Nuns and Novices" by Susan P. Casteras (129-60); "The Female Diaconate in the Anglican Church: What Kind of Ministry for Women?" by Catherine M. Prelinger (161-92); "'Chang-

es Are Dangerous': Women and Temperance in Victorian England" by Lilian Lewis Shiman (193-215); "Respectable Sinners: Salvation Army Rescue Work with Unmarried Mothers, 1884–1914" by Ann R. Higginbotham (216-33); and "The Beginnings of Church Feminism: Women and the Councils of the Church of England, 1897–1919" by Brian Heeney (260-84).

Murdoch, Norman H. "Female Ministry in the Thought and Work of Catherine Booth." *Chrisitan History* 53 (September 1984): 348-62. Well documented.

Power, Eileen. *See above,* Historical Periods: Medieval Period.

Roberts, William. *Memoirs of the Life and Correspondence of Mrs. Hannah More.* 2 vols. New York: Harper & Brothers, 1934.
    Documents from a English writer and activist.

Ross, Isabel. *See below,* Denominations: Quakers.

Rupp, Ernest Gordon. *Religion in England 1688–1791.* Oxford History of the Christian Church series. New York: Oxford University Press, 1986. 584 pp. Includes bibliography, index.
    Includes good discussions of Methodist women, the countess of Huntingdon, Sarah Trimmer, and Hannah More.

Sahgal, Gita and Nira Yuval-Davis. *Refusing Holy Orders: Women and Fundamentalism in Britain.* London: Virago Press, 1992. 244 pp. Includes bibliography and index.
    Nine essays on subjects including African-American churches and Irish Catholicism.

Thompson, Roger. *Women in Stuart England and America: A Comparative Study.* Boston: Routledge and Kegan Paul, 1974.
    "Women and the Puritan Churches" is a thoroughly documented discussion of the role of women in Puritan churches in England and America.

Verbrugge, Rita. "Margaret More Roper's Personal Expression in the 'Devout Woman'." In *Silent but for the Word: Tudor Women as Patrons, Translators, and Writer of Religious Works*, ed. Margaret P. Hanney, 30-42. Kent OH: Kent State University Press, 1985.

Wayne, Valeria. "Some Sad Sentences: Vives' 'Instruction of a Christian Woman'." In *Silent but for the Word: Tudor Women as Patrons, Translators, and Writer of Religious Works*, ed. Margaret P. Hanney, 15-29. Kent OH: Kent State University Press, 1985.

Whitney, Janet. *See below*, Denominations: Quaker.

## Hispanic

Isham, Mary. *See below*, Denominations: Methodist.

Johnson, Suzan D. *See above*, Historical Periods: General History.

Keyes, Francis P. W. *See below*, Denominations: Catholic.

Mirande, Alfredo and Evangelina Enriquez. *La Chicana: The Mexican-American Woman*. Chicago: University of Chicago Press, 1979. 283 pp. Good bibliography.
No chapter on religion but see " Religion" in index for scattered pages that include information regarding the Mexican-American woman's experience with the church.

Webster, John C. B., and Ellen Low. *See above*, Historical Periods: General History.

## Native American

Johnson, Suzan D. *See above*, Historical Periods: General History.

Buehrle, Marie Cecilia. *Kateri of the Mohawks*. Milwaukee: Bruce Publishing Co., 1954. 192 pp.
Biography of a Native American Catholic saint. Although two references are made to sizable bibliographies of her life, none is provided here.

Wisbey, Herbert A. *Pioneer Prophetess: Jemima Wilkinson, the Publick Universal Friend.* Ithaca NY: Cornell University Press, 1964. 232 pp. Includes bibliographic essay, index.
    A nondenominational preacher who founded a religious society.

# Denominations and/or Sects

## Baptist

Allen, Catherine B. *A Century to Celebrate: History of Woman's Missionary Union.* Birmingham AL: Woman's Missionary Union, SBC, 1987. 515 pp. Good documentation, index.
    A thorough, well-organized history of a major missions organization.

Allen, Catherine B. *The New Lottie Moon Story.* Nashville: Broadman Press, 1980. 320 pp. Well documented, bibliography, index.
    A solid biography of a missions pioneer in China.

Anders, Sarah Frances. "Woman's Role in the Southern Baptist Convention and Its Churches as Compared with Selected Other Denominations." *Review and Expositor.* 72 (Winter 1975): 31-39. Good documentation.

Beck, James. R. *See above,* Ethnic-National: British.

Blevins, Carolyn D. "Women in Baptist History." *Review and Expositor.* 83 (Winter 1986): 51-61. Good documentaion.

Brumberg, Joan Jacobs. *Mission for Life: The Story of the Family of Adoniram Judson, and the Dramatic Events of the First American Foreign Mission, and the Course of Evangelical Religion in the Nineteenth Century.* New York: Macmillan, 1980. 302 pp. Voluminous notes, both documentary and explanatory; excellent bibliography.
    Solid account of a significant American missionary family.

Cattan, Louise Armstrong. *Lamps Are for Lighting.* Grand Rapids: Wm. B. Eerdmans, 1972. 123 pp. Documentation, bibliography, index.
    The story of the work of Helen Barrett Montgomery and Lucy Waterbury Peabody in the mission program of American Baptists.

Clement, A. S. *Great Baptist Women*. London: Carey Kingsgate Press, 1955. 116 pp. Undocumented.

Biographical sketches of Dorothy Hazzard, Elizabeth Gaunt, Anne Steele, Hannah Marshman, Mary Carey, Elizabeth Sale, Ann Judson, Henrietta Hall Shuck, Lydia Mary de Hailes, Hettie Rowntree Clifford, and Mary Eleanor Bowser.

Davis, Almond H. *The Female Preacher; Or Memoir of Salome Lincoln*. New York: Arno, 1972. 162 pp. Some explanatory notes, no bibliography or index.

After participating in a labor strike, this 19th-century Free Will Baptist left her work to preach in New England, insisting that in the eyes of God all were equal.

Higginbotham, Evelyn Brooks. *See above*, Ethnic-National: African-American.

Hoadley, Frank T. and Benjamin P. Browne. *Baptists Who Dared*. Valley Forge PA: Judson Press, 1980. 112 pp. Includes bibliography.

Includes discussions of Mary Williams, Ann Judson, Ellen Winsor Cushing, Helen Barrett Montgomery, Jennie Clare Adams, and Thomasine Allen. Very easy reading.

Hyatt, Irwin T., Jr. *See above*, Historical Periods: America: Nineteenth Century.

Jeter, Jeremiah Bell. *A Memoir of Mrs. Henrietta Shuck: The First American Female Missionary to China*. Boston: Gould, Kendall and Lincoln, 1846. 251 pp. No bibliography, no index.

Significant use of primary materials, that is, letters.

Knowles, James D. *Memoir of Mrs. Ann H. Judson*. Women in American Protestant Religion Series: 1800–1930. New York: Garland Press, 1987. Reprint of 1831 edition. 408 pp. No documentation.

Good use of the correspondence from Ann Judson.

Letsinger, Norman Herbert. "The Status of Women in the Southern Baptist Convention in Historical Perspective." *Baptist History and Heritage.* 12/1 (1977): 37-44. Documented.

Lumpkin, William L. "The Role of Women in Eighteenth Century Virginia Baptist Life." *Baptist History and Heritage.* 8:3 (1973): 158-67. Good documentation.

McBeth, Leon. "The Changing Role of Women in Baptist History." *Southwestern Journal of Theology.* 22 (Fall 1979): 84-96. Documented.

_____. *Women in Baptist Life.* Nashville: Broadman Press, 1979. 190 pp. Documentation, suggested readings.
    A history of English and American women in Baptist life from the 17th century to the present.

Montgomery, Helen Barrett. *Helen Barrett Montgomery: From Campus to World Citizenship.* New York NY: Fleming H. Revell, 1940. 141 pp. No bibliography or index.
    Brief biography and tributes from friends.

_____. *Western Women in Eastern Lands: An Outline Study of Fifty Years of Woman's Work in Foreign Missions.* Women in Protestant Religion Series: 1880–1930. New York: Macmillan Co., 1910. 286 pp.

"Role of Women in Baptist History, The." *Baptist History and Heritage* 12/1 (1977).
    The entire issue deals with the topic, and includes the following articles: "The Role of Women in Southern Baptist History" by Leon McBeth (3-25; a capsule of his book—see above); "Baptist Women in Missions Support in the Nineteenth Century" by Helen E. Falls (26-36); "The Status of Women in the Southern Baptist Convention in Historical Perspective" by Norman H. Letsinger (37-44; a capsule of his dissertation); "Southern Baptists and Women's Right to Vote, 1910–1920" by Bill Sumners (45-51); and "Deaconesses in Baptist History: A Preliminary Study" by Charles W. Deweese (52-57).

Sorrill, Bobbie. *Annie Armstrong: Dreamer in Action.* Nashville: Broadman Press, 1984. 320 pp. Well documented, bibliography, index.
An account of the significant contributions of a missions organizer.

Stewart, I. D. *The History of the Freewill Baptists: From 1780 to 1830.* Volume 1. Dover: Freewill Baptist Printing, 1943. Reprint of 1862 document. 416 pp.
Throughout this history women are noted for their effective preaching. Lists of ordained ministers however do not include women. Minimal documentation.

Torbet, Robert G. *Venture of Faith: The Story of the American Baptist Foreign Missionary Society and the Woman's American Baptist Foreign Missionary Society 1814–1954.* Philadelphia: Judson Press, 1955. 634 pp. Well documented, fine bibliography, large index.

Vail, Albert L. *See above,* Historical Periods: America: Nineteenth Century.

"Women in Ministry." *American Baptist* 185/4 (1987).
The entire issue deals with the topic, and includes articles on Mary Webb, Ann Hasseltine Judson, Lulu Fleming, Helen Barrett Montgomery, Kathryn Baker, and several contemporary women.

"Women in Southern Baptist History." *Baptist History and Heritage.* 22/3 (1987).
The entire issue deals with the topic, and includes the following articles: "Shaping of Leadership among Southern Baptist Women" by Carolyn Weatherford (12-20); "Southern Baptist Laywomen in Missions" by Bobbie Sorrill (21-28); "The Impact of Southern Baptist Women on Social Issues: Three Viewpoints" by Rosalie Beck, Kay Shurden, and Catherine Allen (29-40); "Patterns of Ministry among Southern Baptist Women" by Carolyn D. Blevins (41-49); and "Southern Baptist Women as Writers and Editors" by Evelyn Wingo Thompson (50-58).

## Catholic

Boulding, Elise. *The Underside of History: A View of Women through Time.* Boulder CO: Westview Press, 1976.

See "Catholic Pioneers in Europe," 568-70. *See also* Boulding under Ethnic-National: Asian.

Brotherton, Anne, ed. *The Voice of the Turtledove: New Catholic Women in Europe*. New York: Paulist Press. 1992. 217 pp. Documented.
Candid essays by Catholic women from eight European countries expressing the frustrations with the church and their commitment to it.

Buehrle, Marie Cecilia. *See above*, Ethnic-National: Native American.

Burton, Katherine. *His Dear Persuasion: The Life of Elizabeth Ann Seton*. New York: Longmans, Green and Co., 1942. 304 pp. Undocumented, short bibliography.

_____. *In No Strange Land*. Freeport NY: Books for Libraries Press, 1970. 254 pp. Includes bibliography.
Stories of conversions of outstanding Americans to Catholicism: Sarah Worthington King Peter; Sophia Dana Ripley; Lucy Smith (Mother Catherine de Ricci); Rose Hawthorne (Mary Alphonsa) Lathrop (Mother Alphonsa); and Marion Gurney (Mother Marianne of Jesus).

Coles, Robert. *Dorothy Day: A Radical Devotion*. Reading MA: Addison-Wesley Publishing, 1987. 182 pp. Documentation, annotated selected bibliography, index.

Day, Dorothy. *The Long Loneliness: An Autobiography of Dorothy Day*. San Franscisco: Harper & Row, 1981. 288 pp. Index.
Day, a Catholic socialist explains her work and her philosophy.

_____. *Meditations*. New York: Newman Press, 1970. 81 pp.

Day, Helen Caldwell. *See above*, Ethnic-National: African-American.

Dirvin, Joseph I. *Mrs. Seton: Foundress of the American Sisters of Charity*. New York: Farrar, Straus, & Giroux, 1975. 498 pp. Thorough bibliography, fine index.
Biography of Elizabeth Ann (Bayley) Seton.

Doig, Desmond. *Mother Teresa: Her People and Her Work.* New York: Harper & Row, 1976. 175 pp.

Dwyer, Maureen, ed. *New Women, New Church, New Priestly Ministry: Proceedings of the Second Conference on the Ordination of Roman Catholic Women.* Rochester NY: Kirkwood Press. 1980. 178 pp.

Ewens, Mary. *The Role of the Nun in the Nineteenth Century.* New York: Arno Press, 1978. 427 pp. Good bibliography.
   Explains role as defined by canon law and as experienced in first American communities, 1790–1900; discusses the problems and interactions with society.

Flinders, Carol Lee. *Enduring Grace: Living Portraits of Seven Women Mystics.* San Francisco: Harper, 1993. 248 pp. Includes bibliographic regferences, selected bibliography, index.
   Good collection. Fine studies of Clare, Mechthild of Magdeburg, Julian of Norwich, Catherine of Siena, Catherine of Genoa, Teresa of Avila, and Therese of Lisieux.

Ide, Arthur Frederick. *Woman as Priest, Bishop, and Laity in the Early Catholic Church to 440 A.D.* Mesquite TX: Ide House, 1984. 124 pp. Good documentation, index.
   A defense of the active participation of women in early Christianity.

Kenneally, James J. "Eve, Mary, and the Historians: American Catholicism and Women." In *Women in American Religion,* ed. Janet Wilon James, 191-206. Philadelphia: University of Pennsylvania Press, 1980.

_____. *The History of American Catholic Women.* New York: Crossroad Publications, 1990. 286 pp. Well documented with bibliography, index.
   Chronicles Catholic women's contributions as novelists, nuns, "ladies," reformers, wage earners, and suffragists.

Kennelly, Karen, ed. *American Catholic Women: A Historical Exploration.* New York: Macmillan Publishing, 1989. 231 pp. Well documented with index.

Includes discussion of nuns, homemakers, women in work force, reformers, and activists.

Keyes, Frances Parkinson Wheeler *The Rose and the Lily: The Lives and Times of Two South American Saints.* New York: Hawthorn Books, 1961. 253 pp. Includes bibliography.
Rosa of Lima (1586–1617) and Mariana de Jesus (1618–1645).

Klejment, Anne and Alice. *Dorothy Day and "The Catholic Worker": A Bibliography and Index.* New York: Garland Publishing, 1986. 412 pp.
Includes a bilbiography of works by Day, a bibliography about Day and the newspaper, and four indexes. Valuable resource.

Le Joly, Edward. *Mother Teresa of Calcutta.* San Francisco: Harper & Row, 1977. 345 pp. No documentation, no bibliography, no index.

Lord, Bob and Penny. *Saints and Other Powerful Women in the Church.* N.p.: Journeys of Faith, 1989. Little documentation, short bibliography, no index.
Discusses seven saints and three modern women.

Malmgreen, Gail. *See above,* Ethnic-National: British.

Miller, William D. *Dorothy Day: A Biography.* San Francisco: Harper and Row, 1982. 518 pp. No bibliography; good index.

Moll, Helmut, ed. *The Church and Women: A Compendium.* San Francisco: Ignatius Press, 1988. 277 pp. Documented.
Sixteen essays—most theological, some historical.

Muggeridge, Malcolm. *Something Beautiful for God: Mother Teresa of Calcutta.* London: Collins, 1971. 156 pp. Some photos; not the best.

Oates, Mary J. "Organized Voluntarism: The Catholic Sisters in Massachusetts, 1870–1940." In *Women in American Religion,* ed. Janet Wilson James, 141-69. Philadelphia: University of Pennsylvania Press, 1980.

Parbury, Kathleen. *See above,* General Reference.

Ruether, Rosemary R., and Eleanor McLaughlin. *See above*, Historical Periods: General History.

St. Pierre, Simone M. *The Struggle to Serve: The Ordination of Women in the Roman Catholic Church.* Jefferson NC: McFarland & Co., 1994. 203 pp. Well documented, with extensive bibliography and index.
    Challenges arguments in the *Declaration on the Question of the Admission of Women to the Ministerial Priesthood,* a 1976 document of the Roman Catholic Church.

Smith, Betsy Covington. *See above*, Historical Periods: General History.

Sahgal, Gita, and Nira Yuval-Davis. *See above*, Ethnic-National: British.

Swidler, Leonard, and Arlene, eds. *Women Priests: A Catholic Commentary on the Vatican Declaration.* New York: Paulist Press, 1977. 352 pp. Includes bibliographic references.
    Forty-two of the articles address basic issues of women's ordination; several articles deal with historical periods or persons.

Wallace, Ruth A. *They Call Her Pastor: A New Role for Catholic Women.* Series in Religion, Culture, and Society. Albany: State University of New York Press, 1992. 204 pp. Documentation, bibliography, index.
    A study of 20 Catholic parishes administered by women.

Ward, Maisie. *Caryll Houselander: That Divine Eccentric.* New York: Sheed and Ward, 1962. 323 pp. Undocumented.

_____, ed. *The Letters of Caryll Houselander: Her Spiritual Legacy.* New York: Sheed and Ward, 1965. 238 pp.

_____. *Unfinished Business.* New York: Sheed and Ward, 1964. 374 pp.

## Christian Reformed

Grissen, Lillian V., ed. *For Such a Time as This: Twenty-Six Women of Vision and Faith Tell Their Stories.* Grand Rapids: Wm. B. Eerdmans, 1991. 276 pp. No running documentation, but includes bibliography and index.

## Christian Science

Bednarowski, Mary Farrell. *See above*, Historical Periods: America: Nineteenth Century.

Dakin, Franden. *Mrs. Eddy, The Biography of a Virginal Mind.* New York: Charles Scribner's Sons, 1929. 553 pp. Annotated bibliography, extensive index.

Eddy, Mary Baker. *Christian Healing and the People's Idea of God: Sermons Delivered at Boston.* Boston: Allison V. Stewart, 1916. 14 pp.
Includes the texts of two sermons.

_____. *Miscellaneous Writings, 1883–1896.* Boston: Christian Science Publishing Society, 1918. 471 pp.
Includes letters and addresses with assorted other writings.

_____. *Pulpit and Press.* Boston: Allison V. Stewart, 1916. 90 pp.
A dedicatory sermon by Eddy, with readings and hymns, from First Church of Christ, Scientist, Boston, 6 January 1895. Also includes newspaper accounts from 24 papers.

_____. *Science and Health, with Key to the Scriptures.* Boston: Trustees under the Will of Mary Baker G. Eddy, 1875.
Basic doctrines of Christian Science.

Fox, Margery. "Protest in Piety: Christian Science Revisited." *International Journal of Women's Studies* 4 (1978): 401-16.
Documented. Interprets Christian Science as a woman's protest movement of the 19th century.

Peel, Robert. *Mary Baker Eddy: The Years of Discovery.* New York: Holt, Rinehart, and Winston, 1966. 372 pp. Extensive notes, both documentary and explanatory. No bibliography, but good index.
See also additional volumes: *The Years of Trial* and *The Years of Authority* (New York: Holt, Rinehart, and Winston, 1977). Copious notes, bibliographical references, and index.

Powell, Lyman P. *Mary Baker Eddy: A Life-Size Portrait*. Boston: Christian Science Publishing Society, 1950. 350 pp. Well documented, large index.

Silberger, Julius. *Mary Baker Eddy, An Interpretative Biography of the Founder of Christian Science*. Boston: Little, Brown, 1980. 274 pp. Includes bibliographic references, index.

Tucker, Cynthia Grant. *Healer in Harm's Way: Mary Collson, a Clergywoman in Christian Science*. Knoxville TN: University of Tennessee Press, 1994. 214 pp. Documented; good bibliography.

Tucker, Cynthia Grant. *A Woman's Ministry: Mary Collson's Search for Reform as a Unitarian Minister, Hull House Social Worker, and a Christian Scientist Practioner*. American Civilization series. Philadelphia: Temple University Press, 1984. 216 pp. Well documented, bibliography, index.

Wessinger, Catherine. *See above*, Historical Periods: General History.

## Church of the Brethren

Brubaker, Pamela. *She Hath Done What She Could: A History of Women's Participation in the Church of the Brethren*. Elgin IL: Brethren Press, 1985. 222 pp. Primary materials provided in four appendixes. Good documentation, bibliography, and index.

The story of the organized work of the women and their ministry as laypeople, as deacons, and as professional ministers.

Flora, Jerry R. "Ninety Years of Brethren Women in Ministry." *Ashland Theological Journal* 17 (Fall 1984): 4-21. Well documented.

Brief discussions of several women who served the church between 1894 and 1984.

Sachse, Julius Friedrich. *The German Sectarians of Pennsylvania: A Critical and Legendary History of the Ephrata Cloister and the Dunkers*. 2 vols. New York: AMS Press, 1971.

See esp. "The Rule of the Sisterhood," 176-206 in vol. 2.

## Church of God

Smith, John W. V. *Heralds of a Brighter Day: Biographical Sketches of Early Leaders in the Church of God Reformation Movement.* Anderson IN: Gospel Trumpet Co., 1955.
 Of the five biographies, one is of a woman—Nora S. Hunter, founder and first president of the National Woman's Home and Foreign Missionary Society. No documentation.

## Congregational

Blackwell, Antionette Brown. *See* Lucy Stone, under Social Reform/Social Work, for correspondence.

Cazden, Elizabeth. *Antionette Brown Blackwell, Biography.* Old Westbury NY: The Feminist Press, 1983. 315 pp. Well documented. Includes bibliography, index.

Dunn, Mary Maples. "Saints and Sisters: Congregational and Quaker Women in the Early Colonial Period." In *Women in American Religion,* ed. Janet Wilson James, 27-46. Philadelphia: University of Pennsylvania Press, 1980.

Hays, Elinor. *Those Extraordinary Blackwells: The Story of a Journey to a Better World.* New York: Harcourt, Brace, and World, 1967. 349 pp. Includes bibliography, index.
 Predominantly women's stories, including that of Antionette Brown Blackwell.

Lasser, Carol, and Marlene Merrill. *See above,* Historical Periods: America: Nineteenth Century.

Stone, Lucy. *See above,* Historical Periods: America: Nineteenth Century.

"Woman's Place in Religious Meetings." *Congregational Review* (January 1868): 22-29.
 An exposition of 1 Timothy 2:11-15.

## Disciples of Christ

Bailey, Fred A. "Woman's Superiority in Disciple Thought, 1865–1900." *Restoration Quarterly* 23/3 (1980): 151-60.

Hull, Debra B., ed. *Christian Church Women: Shapers of a Movement.* St. Louis: Chalice Press. 1994. 180 pp. Documented, index.

Good history of varied contributions of women in Disciples of Christ: pastors, evangelists, social reformers, authors, leaders, philanthropists, missionaries.

## Eastern Orthodox

Meehan, Brenda. *Holy Women of Russia: The Lives of Five Orthodox Women Offer Spiritual Guidance for Today.* San Francisco: Harper, 1993. 182 pp. Good documentation, selected bibliography, index.

Chronicles the story of Margarita Tuchkova, Anastasiia Logacheva, Matrona Naumovna Popova, Mother Angelina, Abbess Taisiia, and their influence.

## Episcopal

Bozarth-Campbell, Alla. *Womanpriest: A Personal Odyssey.* New York: Paulist Press, 1978. 229 pp.

Autobiographical account of one of the first Episcopalian woman priests.

Corcoran, Theresa, S. C. *Vida Dutton Scudder.* Twayne's United States Authors series. Boston: Twayne Publishers, 1982. 150 pp. Good documentation, large bibliography, index.

Donovan, Mary. *Women Priests in the Episcopal Church: The Experience of the First Decade.* Cincinnati: Forward Movement Publications. 1988. 180 pp.

Brief history leading to ordination of women. Stories of selected clergywomen.

Donovan, Mary Sudman. *A Different Call: Women's Ministries in the Episcopal Church 1850–1920.* Wilton CT: Morehouse-Barlow. 1986. 230 pp. Well documented, good bibliography, index.

Examines both professional and volunteer ministries.

Hamilton, Michael P., and Nancy S. Montgomery, eds. *The Ordination of Women: Pro and Con.* New York: Morehouse-Barlow Co., 1975. 212 pp.
    Men and women, inside and outside the Episcopal church, argue their positions regarding ordination. A historical window to a denominational debate involving women.

Hartley, William and Ellen. *A Woman Set Apart.* New York: Dodd, Mead and Co., 1963. 275 pp. No documentation, no bibliography, no index.
    Biography of Harriet M. Bedell, Episcopal teacher and missionary.

Hewitt, Emily C. and Suzanne R. Hiatt. *Women Priests: Yes or No?* New York: Seabury Press, 1973. 127 pp. Documented.
    See esp. appendix A. "Chronology of Major Anglican Documents and Actions concerning Women in Holy Orders, 1862–1972" and B. "Report of the Joint Commission on Ordained and Licensed Ministries, 1970."

Heyward, Carter. *A Priest Forever: The Formation of a Woman and a Priest.* New York: Harper & Row, 1976. 146 pp. Some documentation.
    Heyward's account of her journey to priesthood in the Episcopal Church.

Malmgreen, Gail. *See above,* Ethnic-National: British.

Murray, Paul. *See above,* Ethnic-National: African-American.

"On the Philadelphia Ordinations." *Christianity and Crisis* 34 (6 Sept 1974).
    Entire issue devoted to the topic.

Raming, Ida. *The Exclusion of Women from the Priesthood: Divine Law or Sex Discrimination?: A Historical Investigation of the Juridical and Doctrinal Foundations of the Code of Canon Law, Canon 968,I.* Metuchen NJ: Scarecrow Press, 1976. 263 pp. Extensive documentation, bibliography, index.

Examines Episcopal church law restricting women, discussing many weaknesses.

Ruether, Rosemary R., and Eleanor McLaughlin. *See above,* Historical Periods: General History.

Smith, Betsy Covington. *See above,* Historical Periods: General History.

Wondra, Ellen K. *Women and the Episcopal Church.* New York: Episcopal Women's Caucus, 1975. Annotated bibliography, topically arranged, includes media.
Dated but valuable.

## Jehovah's Witness

Harrison, Barbara Grizzuti. *Visions of Glory: A History and a Memory of Jehovah's Witnesses.* New York: Simon & Schuster, 1978.
"Waiting for the World to Die" includes discussion of the Jehovah's Witness attitude toward women.

## Lutheran

Ermarth, Margaret Sittler. *See above,* Historical Periods: General History.

Graebner, Alan. "Birth Control and the Lutherans: The Missouri Synod as a Case Study." In *Women in American Religion,* ed. Janet Wilson James, 229-52. Philadelphia: University of Pennsylvania Press, 1980.

Meyer, Ruth Fritz. *Women on a Mission.* St. Louis: Concordia Publishing House, 1967. 300 pp. Documented; large appendix with 50 pages of data; selected bibliography; index.
Story of the Lutheran Women's Missionary League.

Taege, Marlys. *Women in God's Service: Wings.* St. Louis: Lutheran Women's Missionary League, 1991. 309 pp. No bibliography, no index.
The 50th anniversary history of the Lutheran Women's Missionary League of the Lutheran Church, Missiouri Synod.

Young, Rosa. *See above,* Ethnic-National: African-American.

## Mennonite

Cummings, Mary Lou, ed. *Full Circle: Stories of Mennonite Women.* Newton KS: Faith and Life Press, 1978. 204 pp. Photographs included.
Essays on nineteen Mennonite women. Most essays are documented.

Klingelsmith, Sharon. "Women in the Mennonite Church, 1900–1930." *Mennonite Quarterly Review* 54 (July 1980): 163-207. Well-documented survey.

Rempel, Valerie, et al., eds. *Your Daughters Shall Prophesy: Women in Ministry in the Church.* Hillsboro KS: Kindred Press, 1992. 222 pp. No bibliography, no index.
Mostly biblical expositions but does include a chapter on "Women in the Mennonite Brethren Church."

Rich, Elaine Sommers. *Mennonite Women: A Story of God's Faithfulness, 1683–1983.* Scottdale PA: Herald Press, 1983. 257 pp. Good documentation, bibliography, index.
Traces Mennonite women from Anabaptist ancestors. Focuses on the many leaders but also provides annotated listings of lesser known women.

Unrau, Ruth. *Encircled: Stories of Mennonite Women.* Newton KS: Faith and Life Press, 1986. 352 pp. Some documentation, large index.
Accounts of 33 19th- and 20th-century women.

## Methodist

Acornley, John H. *See above,* Ethnic-National: African-American.

Andrews, William L. *See above,* Ethnic-National: African-American.

Brown, Earl Kent. "Standing in the Shadow: Women in Early Methodism." *Nexus* 17 (Spring 1974): 22-31.
*See also* next entry.

_____. *Women of Mr. Wesley's Methodism.* Studies in Women and Religion series 11. New York: Edwin Mellen Press, 1983. 261 pp. Includes bibliography and index.

A discussion of the leadership roles of women in Methodism and short biographical accounts of six women. *See also* previous entry.

Brown, Kenneth O. "'The Worldwide Evangelist': The Life and Work of Martha Inskip." *Methodist History* 21 (July 1983): 179-91.

Brown, Oswald E., and Anna M. Brown. *Life and Letters of Laura Askew Haygood.* Nashville: Methodist Episcopal Church, South, 1904. Repr.: Women in American Protestant Religion series: 1800–1930. New York: Garland Publishing, 1986. 522 pp.

Buoy, Charles Wesley. *Representative Women of Methodism.* New York: Hunt and Eaton, 1893. 476 pp. No documentation, no bibliography, no index.

A series of lectures given in 1891 on the following Methodist women: Susannah Wesley; Selina, Countess of Huntingdon; Mary Bosanquet Fletcher (first deaconess); Katherine Livingston Garrettson; Eliza Garrett; and Lucy Webb Hayes.

Butler, Mrs. F. A. *A History of the Woman's Foreign Missionary Society Methodist Episcopal Church South.* Nashville: M. E. Church, South, 1912. 181 pp. No documentation, some primary material included.

Chandler, Mrs. E. C. *History of the Women's Foreign Missionary Society of the Methodist Protestant Church.* Pittsburg PA: Press of Pierpoint, Switer & Co., 1920. 239 pp. No documentation.

Chilcote, Paul W. *John Wesley and the Women Preachers of Early Methodism* or *She Offered Them Christ: The Early Legacy of Women Preachers in Early Methodism.* American Theological Library Association Monograph series 25. Metuchen NJ: Scarecrow Press. 1991. 373 pp. Ten appendixes (most primary materials); fine bibliography; index.

Examines the experience of women preachers from early revival period to postrevival era.

Chilcote, Paul W. *She Offered Them Christ: The Legacy of Women Preachers in Early Methodism.* Nashville: Abingdon Press, 1993. 144 pp. Annotated bibliography; notes; index.

Includes some background, Wesley's influence upon women, accounts of individual women, the controversy within Methodism.

Cott, Margaret Van. *The Harvest and the Reaper: Reminiscences of Revival Work of Mrs. Maggie Van Cott.* New York: N. Tibbals and Sons, 1876. 360 pp.

Basically autobiographical. Long out of print, but provides insight into the mind and work of a woman evangelist.

Culver, Elsie Thomas. *See above*, Historical Periods: General History.

Dallimore, Arnold A. *Susanna Wesley: The Mother of John and Charles Wesley.* Grand Rapids: Baker Book House, 1993. 176 pp. Includes bibliographic references and index.

Dayton, Donald W., and Lucille Sider Dayton. "'Your Daughters Shall Prophesy': Feminism in the Holiness Movement." *Methodist History* 14 (January 1976): 67-92.

Quite thorough, well documented.

Dougherty, Mary Agnes Theresa. *The Methodist Deaconess, 1885–1918: A Study in Religious Feminism.* Davis CA: University of California Press, 1979. Large bibliography.

Contains a valuable chapter on Lucy Rider Meyer, founder of the deaconess movement, 29-81.

Eltscher, Susan M. *Women in the Wesleyan and United Methodist Traditions: A Bibliography.* Madison NJ: General Commission on Archives and History, United Methodist Church, 1992. 158 pp. Extensive listing by topics, good index.

Foster, John O. *Life and Labors of Mrs. Maggie Newton Van Cott.* Cincinnati: Hitchcock and Walden, 1872. 339 pp. No documentation.

Biographical account of the first woman licensed to preach in the Methodist Episcopal Church. Appendix: 30 pages of press accounts related to Van Cott's ministry.

Gifford, Carolyn de Swarte. *See above*, Historical Periods: America: Twentieth Century.

Harmon, Rebecca Lamar. *Susanna, Mother of the Wesleys*. Nashville: Abingdon Press, 1968. 175 pp. Includes bibliography.

Holley, Marietta. *Samantha Among the Brethren, by Josiah Allen's Wife*. Women in American Protestant Religion series: 1800–1930. New York: Garland Publishing, 1986. Reprint of 1890 edition. 437 pp.
     Insightful fictional account of a Methodist woman's experience in 19th-century Christianity. Easily read.

Holt, Rackham. *See above*, Ethnic-National: African-American.

Horton, Isabelle. *High Adventure: Life of Lucy Rider Meyer*. Women in American Protestant Religion series: 1800–1930. New York: Garland Publishing, 1987. Reprint of 1928 edition. 359 pp. Undocumented.

Howell, Mabel Katherine. *Women and the Kingdom: Fifty Years of Kingdom Building by the Women of the Methodist Episcopal Church South 1878–1928*. Nashville: Cokesbury Press, 1928. 283 pp. Some documentation, short bibliography, no index.

Ingraham, Sarah R. *Walks of Usefulness. Or, Reminiscences of Mrs. Margaret Prior*. Women in American Protestant Religion series: 1800–1930. New York: Garland Publishing, 1987. Reprint of 1843 edition. 324 pp. No bibliography or index.

Isham, Mary. *Valorous Ventures, a Record of Sixty and Six Years of Women's Foreign Missionary Society, Methodist Episcopal Church*. Boston: Woman's Foreign Missionary Society Methodist Episcopal Church, 1936. 446 pp. No bibliography, no index.

Reports on their work in India, China, Japan, Korea, Africa, Burma, Europe and North Africa, Malaya and Sumatra, Mexico, South America, and the Philippines.

Jones, Charles Edwin. *Perfectionist Persuasion: The Holiness Movement and American Methodism, 1867–1936.* American Theological Library Association monograph series 5. Metuchen NJ: Scrarecrow Press, 1974. 242 pp. Includes bibliographic references.
The role and influence of women is integrated into the history. Phoebe Palmer's role is especially prominent.

Krueger, Christine L. *See above*, Historical Periods: America: Nineteenth Century.

Lee, Elizabeth Meredith. *As Among the Methodists: Deaconesses Yesterday, Today, and Tomorrow.* New York: Woman's Division of Christian Service Board of Missions, Methodist Church, 1963. 133 pp. Documented, bibliography, index.
History of the movement, internationally.

Lee, Jarena. *Religious Experiences and Journal of Mrs. Jarena Lee: "A Preachin' Woman."* Nashville: Legacy Publishing, 1991. 146 pp.
A 19th-century African-American Methodist preacher.

Lee, Luther. *Five Sermons and a Tract.* Chicago: Holrad House, 1975. 135 pp. Includes bibliographic references.
Includes "Woman's Right to Preach the Gospel," the ordination sermon for Antionette Brown in 1853.

Leffael, Dolores C., and Janet L. Sims. *See above*, Ethnic-National: African-American.

Loveland, Anne C. "Domesticity and Religion in the Antebellum Period: The Career of Phoebe Palmer." *The Historian* 39 (May 1977): 455-71. Good documentation.

McAfee, Sara J. *See above*, Ethnic-National: African-American.

MacDonell, Mrs. Robert W. *Belle Harris Bennett, Her Life Work.* Nashville: Cokesbury Press, 1928. 297 pp. No documentation, bibliography, or index.

McDowell, John P. *The Social Gospel in the South: The Woman's Home Mission Movement in the Methodist Episcopal Church, South, 1886–1939.* Baton Rouge: Louisana State University Press, 1982. 167 pp. Documented, fine bibliography, index.

McQuaid, Ina DeBord. *A Lady of High Wycombe.* New York: Vantage Press, 1964. 160 pp. Includes bibliography.
     Story of Hannah Ball, an English Methodist early leader of Sunday Schools. Of special interest is appendix 1, which is 43 letters to Hannah from John Wesley.

Martin, Margaret. *Heroines of Early Methodism.* Nashville: A. H. Redford, 1875. 224 pp. No documentaion, bibliography, or index.
     A small 4x6 book with large print, so information is brief. Includes Susanna Wesley, Mrs. Fletcher, Mrs. Coke, Lady Huntingdon, Hester Ann Roe Rogers, Lady Maxwell, and Grace Murray.

Meeker, Ruth Esther. *Six Decades of Service, 1880–1940: A History of the Woman's Home Missionary Society of the Methodist Episcopal Church.* Woman's Home Missionary Society of the Methodist Episcopal Church, 1969. 405 pp. Index.
     Contents divided into three parts: the decades, their projects, their methods of work. An extensive examination.

Mitchell, Norma Taylor. "From Social to Radical Feminism: A Survey of Emerging Diversity in Methodist Women's Organizations, 1869–1974." *Methodist History* 13 (April 1975): 21-44.

Morrow, Thomas M. *Methodist Women.* London: Epworth Press, 1967. 119 pp. Undocumented.
     Focuses at length on Sarah Crosby, Hannah Ball, Frances Pawson, Mary Fletcher, and Sarah Bentley.

Newton, John Anthony. *Susanna Wesley and the Puritan Tradition in Methodism*. London: Epworth, 1968. 215 pp. Includes bibliography, index.
A good biography of Wesley.

Noll, William T. "Women as Clergy and Laity in the 19th Century Methodist Protestant Church." *Methodist History* 15 (January 1977): 107-21.

Norwood, Frederick A., ed. *Sourcebook of American Methodism*. Nashville: Abingdon Press, 1982. 683 pp.
The section "Women Find a Voice" (444-75) includes eleven primary documents from the 19th and early 20th century.

Palmer, Phoebe. *Promise of the Father*. Higher Christian Life series. New York: Garland Publishing, 1985. Reprint of 1859 edition. 421 pp.
Strong defense of women in church work.

————. *Phoebe Palmer: Selected Writings*. Sources of American Spirituality series. New York: Paulist Press, 1988. 364 pp. Good explanatory notes, fine bibliography, indexes.

Raser, Harold E. *Phoebe Palmer: Her Life and Thought*. Studies in Women and Religion 22. Lewiston NY: Edwin Mellen Press, 1987. 389 pp. Extensive notes, valuable bibliography, index.
Good examination of Palmer's contributions, making significant use of Palmer's writings.

Rowe, Kenneth E. *See above*, General Reference.

Ruether, Rosemary R., and Eleanor McLaughlin. *See above*, Historical Periods: General History.

Rupp, Ernest Gordon. *See above*, Ethnic-National: British.

Smith, Betsy Covington. *See above*, Historical Periods: General History.

Stevens, Abel. *The Women of Methodism: Its Three Foundresses, Susan Wesley, the Countess of Huntingdon, and Barbara Heck, with Sketches of Their Female Associates and Successors in the Early History of the Denomination.* Women in American Protestant Religion series: 1800–1930. New York: Garland Press, 1987. Reprint of 1869 document. 304 pp.

> Deals primarily with Wesley and Heck. Appendix: Documents of American Ladies Centenary Movement.

Tatun, Noreen Dunn. *A Crown of Service: A Story of Woman's Work in the Methodist Episcopal Church, South, from 1878 to 1940.* Nashville: Parthenon Press, 1960. 418 pp. Includes bibliographic notes, good index.

> Chronicles their missionary work.

Thoburn, J. M. *Life of Isabella Thoburn.* Women in American Protestant Religion series: 1880–1930. New York: Garland Publishing, 1987. Reprint of 1903 document. 373 pp.

> Thoburn was a Methodist missionary to India.

Thomas, Hilah F., and Rosemary Skinner Keller, eds. *Women in New Worlds: Historical Perspectives on the Wesleyan Tradition.* Nashville: Abingdon Press, 1981. 445 pp. Thoroughly documented.

> Essays cover a wide range of topics: women in Wesley's Methodism, Phoebe Palmer, Frances Willard, Mary McLeod Bethune, Georgia Harkness, minister's wives, frontier and hispanic, schools, deaconesses, laity, preachers, temperance, industrial reform, Korean independence, and Winifred L. Chappell. For vol. 2, see Keller, *Women in New Worlds.*

Tucker, Ruth A. *See above*, Historical Periods: General History.

Wheatley, Richard. *The Life and Letters of Mrs. Phoebe Palmer.* Higher Christian Life series. New York: Garland Publishing, 1984. Reprint of 1881 edition. 636 pp.

White, Mary Culler. *The Days of June.* Nashville: Woman's Board of Foreign Missions, Methodist Episcopal Church, South, 1909. 128 pp.

> An account of Culler's experiences in China.

————. *The Portal of Wonderland: The Life Story of Alice Culler Cobb.* Women in American Protestant Religion series: 1800–1930. New York: Garland Publishing, 1987. Reprint of 1925 document. 240 pp. No documentation.

   Biography of Cobb detailing her role in education and missions.

Willard, Frances Elizabeth Caroline. *Woman in the Pulpit* (1882). Repr.: in *The Defense of Women's Rights to Ordination in the Methodist Episcopal Church.* Ed. Carolyn De Swarte Gifford. New York: Garland Publishing, 1987. 238 pp.

   Gifford's editorial introduction includes a sketch of John Wesley's endorsement of women preachers and of selected Methodist women preachers. Willard's 167-page defense charges that male ministers do not want to share their ecclesiastical power and will risk the loss of women in the Methodist church if they do not. Willard's document is followed by a writing of William F. Warren, a Methodist minister and president of Boston University, who argues for male and female copastors.

## Moravian

Fries, Adelaide Lisetta. *The Road to Salem.* Chapel Hill: University of North Carolina Press, 1944. 316 pp.

   Includes the story of Anna Catharina Ernst.

Myers, Elizabeth Lehman. *A Century of Moravian Sisters: A Record of Christian Community Life.* New York: Fleming H. Revell, 1918. 243 pp. No documentation, bibliography, or index.

## Mormon (Church of Jesus Christ of Latter-day Saints)

Arrington, Leonard J., and Davis Britton. *The Mormon Experience: A History of the Latter-Day Saints.* New York: Alfred A. Knopf, 1979. 404 pp. Includes index.

   See the chapter "Mormon Sisterhood: Charting the Changes," which examines women's role.

Brunson, Madelon. *Bonds of Sisterhood: A History of the RLDS Women's Organization, 1842–1983.* Independence MO: Herald Publishing House. 1985. 170 pp. Documented appendixes; bibliography.

RLDS is the splinter group Reorganized Church of Jesus Christ of Latter-Day Saints.

Conway, Jill K. *See above*, General Reference.

Ellsworth, S. George, ed. *Dear Ellen: Two Mormon Women and Their Letters*. Salt Lake City: University of Utah Library, 1974. 92 pp. Good index.
    Correspondence between two Mormon women. Chief interest is family life.

Foster, Lawrence. *See below*, Denominations: Shakers (both listings).

Fryer, Judith. *See below*, Denominations: Oneida Community.

Hartshorn, Leon R. *Remarkable Stories from the Lives of Latter-Day Saint Women*. Salt Lake City: Desert Books Co., 1974. 274 pp. Some documentation, index.
    Includes the writings of 47 women, biographical sketches of some, photos of some.

Holzapfel, Richard and Jeni. *Women of Nauvoo*. Salt Lake City: Bookcraft, 1992. 225 pp. Well documented, bibliography, good index.
    The work of Mormon women in Commerce, Illinois.

Kern, Louis J. *See below*, Denominations: Shakers.

Mulder, William, and A. Russell Mortensen, eds. *Among the Mormons: Historic Accounts by Contemporary Observers*. New York: Alfred A. Knopf, 1958. 482 pp.
    Includes articles and letters by Mormon women.

Wallace, Irving. *The Twenty-Seventh Wife*. New York: Simon & Schuster, 1961. 443 pp. Includes bibliography.
    This is the story of Ann Eliza Young, wife of Brigham Young.

Young, Ann Eliza Webb. *Wife No. 19*. American Women: Images and Realities series. New York: Arno Press, 1972. 605 pp.
    Discusses the difficulties of polygamy.

Young, Kimball. *Isn't One Wife Enough?* New York: Henry Holt, 1954. 476 pp.

Three views of Mormon polygamy. A sociological analysis of the relationships of family members and the controversy surrounding Mormon polygamy in America.

## Oneida Community

Foster, Lawrence. *See below,* Denominations: Shakers (both listings).

Fryer, Judith. "American Eves in American Edens." *American Scholar* 44 (Winter 1975): 78-99.

Roles and concepts of women in Oneida communities, the Shakers, and the Mormons.

Kern, Louis J. *See below,* Denominations: Shakers.

Yambura, Barbara S., with Eunice W. Bodine. *A Change and a Parting: My Story of Amana.* Ames: Iowa State University Press, 1960. 361 pp.

A personal account of life in an utopian community.

## Pentecostal

LaBerge, Agnes N. O. *What God Hath Wrought: Life and Work of Mrs. Agnes N. O. LaBerge.* Higher Christian Life series. New York: Garland Press, 1985. 127 pp.

Personal account of a Pentecostal evangelist.

Lawless, Elaine J. *God's Peculiar People: Women's Voices and Folk Tradition in a Pentecostal Church.* Lexington KY: University Press of Kentucky, 1988. 159 pp. Documented, large bibliography, index.

Focuses primarily on southern Indiana.

————. *Handmaidens of the Lord: Pentecostal Women and Traditional Religion.* Philadelphia: University of Pennsylvania Press, 1988. 272 pp. Large appendix of sermon texts, extensive bibliography, index.

Tells life stories and examines themes of the ministries of white Pentecostals in Missouri.

_____. *Pentecostal Women Preachers and Traditional Religion.* Philadelphia: University of Pennsylvania Press, 1988. 272 pp. Well documented, extensive bibliography, index.

Examines life stories of the preachers, common themes in their sermons. Includes sermon texts.

Warner, Wayne E. *The Woman Evangelist: The Life and Times of Charismatic Evangelist Maria B. Woodworth-Etter.* Studies in Evangelicalism series 8. Metuchen NJ: Scarecrow Press, 1986. 340 pp. Primary documents in appendixes. Includes bibliography, index.

Fine example of a woman Pentecostal preacher.

Wessinger, Catherine. *See above,* Historical Periods: General History.

White, Alma. *Looking Back from Beulah.* Women in American Protestant Religion series: 1800–1930. New York: Garland Publishing, 1987. Reprint of 1902 document. 384 pp. Includes photos.

Explains the calling and work of White as a founder of the Pillar of Fire Church and a worldwide evangelist.

White, Charles Edward. *The Beauty of Holiness: Phoebe Palmer as Theologian, Revivalist, Feminist, and Humanitarian.* Grand Rapids: Francis Asbury Press, 1986. 330 pp. Useful appendixes, extensive notes, fine bibliography, index.

A biography that also analyzes Palmer's teachings in the context of her times.

## Presbyterian

Bethune, Joanna. *See below,* Social Reform.

Boyd, Lois A., and R. Douglas Brackenridge. *Presbyterian Women in America: Two Centuries of a Quest for Status.* Westport CT: Greenwood Press, 1983. 308 pp. Thoroughly documented, extensive bibliography, fine index.

Covers period of 1789–1958. Describes organizations and ordinations of Presbyterian women. Examines contributions of both professional and laywomen. Assesses the contemporary situation for women.

Charteris, A. H. "Woman's Work in the Church" in *Presbyterian Review* (April 1888): 285-92.
Supports the organization of women's work.

Foote, Cheryl J. "Alice Blake of Trementina: Mission Teacher of the Southwest." *Journal of Presbyterian History* 60 (Fall 1982): 228-42. Documented account.

Irvine, Mary D., and Alice L. Eastwood. *Pioneer Women of the Presbyterian Church, United States.* Richmond: Presbyterian Committee of Publication, 1923. 399 pp. No documentation, bibliography, or index.
Chronicles the birth of the Woman's Auxiliary of the Southern Presbyterian Church. Majority of text devoted to histories of the state organizations, includes 16 state histories.

Penfield, Janet Harbison. "Women in the Presbyterian Church: An Overview." *Journal of Presbyterian History* 55 (Summer 1977): 107-23. Well-documented survey.

Stephenson, P. D. "The Woman Question." *Presbyterian Quarterly* (April 1899): 206-28 and (October 1899): 685-724.
Opposes woman's expanding role in church and society.

Verdesi, Elizabeth Howell. *In But Still Out: Women in the Church.* Philadelphia: Westminster Press, 1976. 218 pp. Good documentation, good bibliography.
An account and analysis of the loss of power in the 1920s and again in the 1940s and 1950s.

Wilson, Carol Green. *Chinatown Quest.* San Francisco: California Historical Society, 1974. 189 pp. Undocumented.
Recounts the impact of Donaldina Cameron's work at the Chinese Presbyterian Mission Home in San Francisco from 1895 to 1938. Cameron's work focused on rescuing Chinese slave girls and training them for a new life.

## Quaker

Bacon, Margaret H. *As the Way Opens: The Story of Quaker Women in America.* Richmond IN: Friends United Press, 1980. 128 pp. No documentation.
Chronicles Quaker women's role in ministry, education, the professions, reform movements, and the peace movement.

Barbour, Hugh. *Mary Fell Speaking.* Wallingford PA: Pendle Hill, 1976. Pamphlet #206.
Brief autobiography, three letters, and a 1666 tract on women speaking.

Best, Mary Agnes. *Rebel Saints.* Freeport NY: Books for Libraries Press, 1968. Reprint of 1925 edition. 333 pp. Includes bibliography.
Includes chapters on Margaret Fell, Mary Fisher, Katherine Evans, Sarah Chevers, Mary Dyer, and Elizabeth Haddon.

Birney, Catherine H. *See below,* Social Reform.

Brailsford, Mabel Richmond. *Quaker Women, 1650–1690.* London: Ducksworth and Co., 1915. 340 pp. Brief bibliography, short index.
George Fox's influence on women, discussions of Margaret Fell and other women in England, Ireland, and Holland. Out of print but valuable.

Chace, Elizabeth Buffum. *Two Quaker Sisters.* New York: Liveright Publishing Co., 1937. 183 pp.
The story of Lucy Buffum Lovell and Elizabeth Buffum Chace, including the antislavery reminiscences of Elizabeth.

Dieter, Melvin E. "The Smiths—a Biographical Sketch with Selected Items from the Collection." *Asbury Seminarian* 38 (Spring 1983): 6-41. Includes primary materials and photos of documents. Short selected bibliography.
On Hannah Whitall Smith.

Drinker, Sopie Hutchinson. *Hannah Penn and the Proprietorship of Pennsylvania.* Philadelphia: National Society of the Colonial Dames of America in the Commonwealth of Pennsylvania, 1958. 207 pp. Includes documents concerning Hannah Penn, bibliography, index.
    Significant use of correspondence of Hannah, second wife of William Penn.

Dunn, Mary Maples. "Women of Light." In *Women of America: A History,* ed. Carol Ruth Berkin and Mary Beth Norton. Boston: Houghton-Mifflin, 1979.
    Discusses woman's experience in the Quaker faith and concludes with six documents.

Evans, W. and T. *Friends Library.* 14 vols. Philadelphia: Joseph Rakestraw, 1837. Includes primary materials, index.
    Excellent materials on early Quaker women.

Fell, Margaret. *Women's Speaking Justified.* The Augustan Reprint Society publication no. 194. Los Angeles: William Andrews Clark Memorial Library, University of California, 1979. Reprint of 1667 document. 22 pp. Includes bibliographic references.

Fornell, Ear W. *The Unhappy Medium: Spiritualism and the Life of Margaret Fox.* Austin: University of Texas Press, 1964. 204 pp. Good bibliography, index.
    Focuses on Fox as a medium.

Kunze, Bonnelyn Young. *Margaret Fell and the Rise of Quakerism.* London: Macmillan, 1994. 327 pp. Extensive notes, very good bibliography, index.
    Explores the domestic, economic, political, and religious world of Fell and her personal response to it, and her contributions to both issues of gender and sects.

Leach, Robert J. *Women Ministers: A Quaker Contribution.* Pendle Hill Pamphlet 227. Lebanon PA: Sowers Printing Co., 1979. 29 pp. No documentation, no bibliography, no index.

Luder, Hope Elizabeth. *Women and Quakerism.* Wallingford PA: Pendle Hill Publishing, 1976. 36 pp. Documented, bibliography.

Malmgreen, Gail. *See above,* Ethnic-National: British.

Manners, Emily. *Elizabeth Hooten: First Quaker Woman Preacher (1600–1672).* London: Headley Brothers, 1914. 95 pp. Documented, bibliography, index.

Mott, Lucretia. *Lucretia Mott: Her Complete Speeches and Sermons.* Ed. Dana Greene. New York: Edwin Mellen Press, 1980. 401 pp. Includes bibliographic references.

Noever, Janet Hubly. "Passionate Rebel: The Life of Mary Gove Nichols, 1810–1884." Ann Arbor MI: University Microfilms International, 1983. 348 pp. Excellent documentation, extensive bibliography.
A facsimile of Noever's dissertation.

Ross, Isabel. *Margaret Fell, Mother of Quakerism.* New York: Longmans, Green, 1949. 421 pp.
The section "Principal sources and books of reference" is a valuable resource.

Ruether, Rosemary R., and Eleanor McLaughlin. *See above,* Historical Periods: General History.

Smith, Hannah Whitall. *The Christian's Secret of a Happy Life.* Westwood NJ: Revell, 1952. 248 pp.

_____. *Philadelphia Quaker: The Letters of Hannah Whitall Smith.* Ed. Logan Pearsall Smith. New York: Harcourt, Brace, and Co., 1950. 234 pp. Some explanatory notes, index.

_____. *A Religious Rebel: The Letters of "H.W.S." (Mrs. Pearsall Smith).* London: Nisbet, 1949. 232 pp.

West, Jessamyn. *The Quaker Reader.* New York: Viking Press, 1962. 522 pp. Good bibliography.

Includes writings of Mary Penington, Margaret Fell, Elizabeth Fry, Caroline Fox, Elizabeth Buffum Chace, Teresina R. Havens, Nora Waen, A. Ruth Fry, Hannah Whitall Smith, Helen Thomas Flexner, Elizabeth Gray Vining, and Caroline Stephen.

Whitney, Janet. *Elizabeth Fry, Quaker Heroine.* London: Harrap & Co., 1937. 328 pp. Some illustrations, bibliography, index. *Also* British.

## Seventh-Day Adventist

Delafield, D. A. *Ellen G. White and the Seventh-Day Adventist Church.* Mountain View CA: Pacific Press, 1963. 90 pp. Brief undocumented biography.

Noorbergen, Rene. *Ellen G. White: Prophet of Destiny.* New Canaan CT: Keats Publishing, 1972. 241 pp. Documented, limited bibliography.

Numbers, Ronald L. *Prophetess of Health: Ellen G. White and the Origins of Seventh-Day Adventist Health Reform.* Knoxville: University of Tennessee Press, 1992. 335 pp. Extensive notes including bibliographic references, good index.

White, Ellen G. *See above,* General Reference.

White, Ellen Gould Harmon. *The Great Controversy between Christ and Satan, the Conflict of the Ages in the Christian Dispensation.* Nashville: Southern Publishing Association, 1911. 802 pp.
    Traces the history of the struggles beginning with the destruction of Jerusalem and the early church to the modern era.

————. *The Ministry of Healing.* Mountain View CA: Pacific Press Publishing Assocation, 1942. 540 pp.
    Presents the rationale for her concept of health and its practical implications.

————. *Steps to Christ.* Washington DC: Washington Review and Herald Pubishing Association, 1921. 128 pp.

## Shakers

Andrews, Edward Deming. *People Called Shakers: A Search for the Perfect Society*. New York: Oxford University Press, 1953. 309 pp. Large collection of primary documents in the appendixes. Includes bibliography, index.

Bednarowski, Mary Farrell. *See above*, Historical Periods: America: Nineteenth Century.

Campbell, D'Ann. "Women's Life in Utopia: The Shaker Experiment in Sexual Equality Reappraised, 1810–1860." *New England Quarterly* 51 (March 1978): 23-38. Good documentation.

Campion, Nardi Reeder. *Ann the Word: The Life of Mother Ann Lee, Founder of the Shakers*. Boston: Little, Brown and Co., 1976. 208 pp. Some photos and illustrations included. Undocumented, bibliography, index.

Carr, Frances A. "Lucy Wright: The First Mother in the Revelation and Order of the First Organized Church." *Shaker Quarterly* 15/3 (1987): 93-100 and 15/4 (1987): 128-31.

Desroche, Henri. *The American Shakers: from Neo-Christianity to Presocialism*. Amherst: University of Massachusetts Press, 1971. 357 pp. Includes bibliographic references.
　　See "Distinguishing between the Church and the World: Ascetic Feminism," 139-84.

Evans, Frederick William. *Ann Lee, The Founder of the Shakers: A Biography*. Mt. Lebanon NY: F. W. Evans, 1858. 187 pp. No documentation, no bibliography, no index.
　　Chap. 9 focuses on Ann Lee; chap. 14 includes a brief discussion of Lucy Wright. Of limited value.

Falk, Nancy A., and Rita M. Gross. *See above*, Historical Periods: General History.

Foster, Lawrence. *Religion and Sexuality: The Shakers, the Mormons, and the Oneida Community*. Urbana: University of Illinois Press, 1984. 363 pp. Includes bibliographic references, index.

    Examines religious communities from a broad perspective. The chapter "Radical Products of the Great Revivals: Reflections on Religion, the Family, and Social Change" includes sections on women and the structure of religious authority.

_____. *Women, Family, and Utopia: Communal Experiments of the Shakers, the Oneida Community, and the Mormons*. Syracuse NY: Syacuse University Press, 1991. 353 pp. Includes bibliographic references, index.

    Solid exploration of women's roles and the communities' attitudes toward women.

Fryer, Judith. *See above*, Denominations: Oneida Community.

Green, Calvin, and Seth Y. Wells, eds. *A Summary View of the Millennial Church*. New York: AMS Press, 1973. 384 pp. Includes bibliographic references.

    Explains the origins and basic doctrines of Shakerism.

Humez, Jean M. *Mother's First-Born Daughters*. Indianapolis: Indiana University Press, 1993. 294 pp. Outstanding bibliography, index.

    A collection of Shaker documents that focuses primarily on Ann Lee and Lucy Wright, but also includes other writings.

_____. *See above*, Ethnic-National: African-American.

Jackson, Rebecca. *See above*, Ethnic-National: African-American.

Kern, Louis J. *An Ordered Love: Sex Roles and Sexuality in Victorian Utopias: the Shakers, the Mormons, and the Oneida Community*. Chapel Hill: University of North Carolina Press, 1981. 430 pp. Extensive notes, large bibliography including many primary sources, index.

    These three groups are examined individually and also assessed collectively. Evaluates the effects of each ideology on woman's role and status.

Melcher, Marguerite F. *The Shaker Adventure*. Princeton NJ: Princeton University Press, 1941. 319 pp. Includes bibliography and index.
 Significant portion devoted to discussion of Ann Lee.

Morse, Flo. *The Shakers and the World's People*. Hanover NH: University Press of New England, 1980. 381 pp. Extensive, chronologically arranged bibliography. Index.
 A combination of primary extracts and history. First section focuses on Ann Lee.

_____. *The Story of the Shakers*. Woodstock VT: Countrymen Press, 1986. 109 pp. Several good photographs. A valuable listing of the locations of collections of Shakers materials. Suggested readings included nonfiction and fiction. Index.
 Brief account of the sect.

Sasson, Diane. *The Shaker Spiritual Narrative*. Knoxville: University of Tennessee Press, 1983. 232 pp. Includes bibliography, index.
 Includes autobiographies of Jane Blanchard and Rebecca Jackson.

Wessinger, Catherine. *See above*, Historical Periods: General History.

Williams, Richard E. *Called and Chosen: The Story of Mother Rebecca Jackson and the Philadelphia Shakers*. American Theological Library Association series 17. Metuchen NJ: Scarecrow Press, 1981. 179 pp. Includes documentation, appendixes, bibliography, index.
 The story of a African-American Shaker preacher.

## Unitarian (*see also* Universalist)

Cazden, Elizabeth. *See above*, Denominations: Congregational.

Conway, Jill K. *See above*, General Reference.

Hays, Elinor. *See above*, Denominations: Congregational.

Meltzer, Milton. *See below*, Social Reform.

Tucker, Cynthia Grant. *Prophetic Sisterhood: Liberal Women Ministers of the Frontier, 1880–1930.* Boston: Beacon Press, 1994. Reprint of 1990 edition. 298 pp. Well documented, excellent bibliography, index.
Group biography of 21 Unitarian women. Examines their methods and relationship to institutions.

———. *A Woman's Ministry. See above,* Denominations: Christian Science.

## United Brethren

Sexton, Lydia. *Autobiography of Lydia Sexton, The Story of Her Life.* Women in American Protestant Religion series: 1800–1930. New York: Garland Press, 1987. Reprint of 1882 edition. 655 pp. 655 pp.

## Universalist (*see also* Unitarian)

Brown, Olympia. The entire 1963 issue of the *Annual Journal of the Universalist Historical Society* is devoted to the career of Brown.

———. *Suffrage and Religious Principles: Speeches and Writings of Olympia Brown.* Ed. Dana Greene. Metuchen NJ: Scarecrow Press, 1983. 182 pp. Includes bibliography, index.
Includes material on women and the church.

———. *Olympia Brown: An Autobiography.* Ed. Gwedolen B. Willis. Racine WI: n.p., 1960. 55 pp.
Personal account of her experience in ministry and the woman's suffrage movement.

Cote, Charlotte. *Olympia Brown: The Battle for Equality.* Racine WI: Mother Courage Press, 1988. 216 pp. Useful appendixes of primary materials. Well documented, no bibliography, good index.

Greene, Dana, ed. *Suffrage and Religious Principle: Speeches and Writings of Olympia Brown.* Metuchen NJ: Scarecrow Press, 1983. 182 pp. Includes bibliography and index.

Hitchings, Catherine F. *Universalist and Unitarian Women Ministers.* Boston: Unitarian Universalist Historical Society. 1985. 179 pp. Index.
Biographical dictionary. Excellent resource.

## Hymn Writers

Carlson, Betty, and Jane S. Smith. *Favorite Women Hymn Writers*. Wheaton: Crossway Books. 1990. 128 pp. Short bibliography, index.
A short chapter on each of twenty women.

Crosby, Fanny J. *Fanny J. Crosby: An Autobiography*. Grand Rapids: Baker Book House, 1989. 270 pp.

Malmgreen, Gail. *See above*, Ethnic-National: British.

Prentiss, George L. *See above*, Historical Periods: American: Nineteenth Century.

Ruffin, Bernard. *Fanny Crosby*. Toronto: United Church Press, 1976. 255 pp. Documented, no bibliography, no index.
Makes good use of Crosby papers for sources.

## Social Reform/Social Work

Anthony, Susan B. *See above*, Historical Periods: America: Nineteenth Century.

Barnes, Gilbert H., and Dwight L. Dumond. *See above*, Historical Periods: America: Nineteenth Century.

Bethune, Joanna. *The Power of Faith Exemplified in the Life and Writings of the Late Mrs. Isabella Graham*. Women in American Protestant Religion Series: 1800–1930. New York: Garland Publishing, 1986. Reprint of 1843 tract.
Includes some correspondence, devotionals, and other writings.

Birney, Catherine H. *The Grimke Sisters: Sarah and Angeline Grimke, the First American Women Advocates of Abolition and Woman's Rights*. New York: Haskell House Publishers, 1970. Undocumented.
Deals with spiritual struggles and religious changes of the sisters.

Blocker, Jack S. *"Give to the Winds Thy Fears": The Women's Temperance Crusade, 1873–1874.* Contributions in Women's Studies series. Westport CT: Greenwood Press, 1985. 280 pp. Documentation, four appendixes, bibliography, index.
    Solid account of the beginnings of the women's temperance movement.

Booth, Catherine. *See above,* Ethnic-National: British.

Booth, Catherine (Munford). *See above,* Ethnic-National: British.

Booth-Tucker, F. de L. *See above,* Ethnic-National: British.

Bordin, Ruth Birgitta Anderson. *Frances Willard: A Biography.* Chapel Hill: University of North Carolina Press, 1986. 294 pp. Well documented, bibliography, index.

———. *Woman and Temperance: The Quest for Power and Liberty, 1873–1900.* American Civilization series. Philadelphia: Temple University Press, 1981. 221 pp. Includes bibliographic references, index.
    History of the Women Christian's Temperance Union, its rise, impact and decline.

Brown, Olympia. *See above,* Denominations: Universalists (three listings).

Coles, Robert. *See above,* Denominations: Catholic.

Earhart, Mary. *Frances Willard: From Prayers to Politics.* Chicago: University of Chicago Press, 1944. 417 pp. Documented, fine bibliography, index.

Epstein, Barbara L. *See above,* Historical Periods: America: Nineteenth Century.

Gordon, Elizabeth Putnam. *Women Torch Bearers: The Story of the Woman's Christian Temperance Union.* Evanston IL: National Woman's Christian Temperance Union, 1924. 320 pp.

Kraditor, Aileen S. *The Ideas of the Woman Suffrage Movement: 1890–1920.* New York: Norton Press, 1980.
"Woman Suffrage and Religion," 75-95, is a concise discussion of the varying attitudes of the suffragists toward religion.

McKinley, Edward H. *Marching to Glory: The History of the Salvation Army in the United States of America, 1880–1980.* San Francisco: Harper & Row, 1980. 286 pp. Bibliographic references, index.
Documents the role of women, esp. Catherine Booth and Evangeline C. Booth.

McLoughlin, William G. *Revivals, Awakenings, and Reform: An Essay on Religion and Social Change in America, 1607–1977.* Chicago: University of Chicago Press, 1978. 239 pp. Good bibliography, index.
Scattered passages on women and revivalism.

Malmgreen, Gail. *See above*, Ethnic-National: British.

Marshall, Helen E. *Dorothea Dix: Forgotten Samaritan.* Chapel Hill: University of North Carolina Press, 1967. Reprint of 1937 edition. 298 pp. Well documented, large bibliography, index.

Meltzer, Milton. *Tongue of Flame: The Life of Lydia Maria Child.* New York: Thomas Y. Crowell, 1965. 210 pp. Includes bibliography, index.
A biography using Child's writings, esp. her correspondence. Text undocumented. Bibliographic listings include locations of Child's papers, works by Child, as well as books about her and her era. *Also* Unitarian.

Merriam, Eve, ed. *Growing Female in America: Ten Lives.* New York: Dell Publishing, 1971. 308 pp. Includes bibliography.
See esp. the chapter on Dr. Anna Howard Shaw (1847–1919) a minister and activist, autobiographical account.

Murdoch, Norman H. *See above*, Ethnic-National: British.

Nation, Carry A. *The Use and Need of the Life of Carry A. Nation.* Topeka: F. M. Steves and Sons, 1905. 201 pp.

Stewart, Eliza Daniel. *Memories of the Crusade: A Thrilling Account of the Great Uprising of the Women of Ohio in 1873, against the Liquor Crime.* Chicago: H. J. Smith, 1890. 535 pp.
    Limited value.

Tyrell, Ian R. *Woman's World/Woman's Empire: The Woman's Christian Temperance Union in International Perspective, 1880–1930.* Chapel Hill: University of North Carolina Press, 1991. 381 pp. Extensive documentation, large index.

Willard, Frances Elizabeth. *Glimpses of Fifty Years: The Autobiography of an American Woman.* Chicago: Woman's Temperance Publication Association, 1889. 704 pp.
    A valuable account.

Willard, Frances Elizabeth. *Women and Temperance: Or, The Work and Workers of the Woman's Christian Temperance Union.* Hartford CT: Park Publishing Co., 1883. 648 pp.

Wilson, Elizabeth. *Fifty Years of Association Work Among Young Women, 1866–1916: A History of Young Women's Christian Association in the United States of America.* Women in American Protestant Religion series: 1800–1930. New York: National Board of the YWCA of the United States of America, 1916. 402 pp. Appendixes contain useful data.
    Includes photos, bibliography, index.

Wilson, Otto, and Robert South Barrett. *Fifty Years Work with Girls, 1883–1933: A Story of the Florence Crittenton Homes.* Alexandria VA: National Florence Crittenton Mission, 1933. 513 pp. Little documentation, index.

# Index of Names

Includes authors of mentioned-only titles and descriptions. When a person is referred to more than once on a page, the page number is given as many times as she or he is mentioned on that page.

Abelard, 24
Adams, Jennie Clare, 73
Addams, Jane, 40
d'Albrecht, Jeanne, 35
Allen, Thomasine, 73
Angelina, Mother, 83
Anne of Jesus, 16
Anthony, Susan B, 49
Aquinas, 7, 25
Armstrong, Annie, 75
Augustine, 7, 19, 22

Baader, Franz von, 7
Baker, Harriet A, 61
Baker, Katherine, 75
Ball, Hannah, 91, 91
Barth, Karl, 7
Bathilda, 6
Beatrice of Nazareth, 26, 26
Beaumont, Agnes, 66
Bedell, Harriet M., 84
Beecher, Catherine, 51, 54
Beecher, Eunice, 15
Bellinger, Mary Ann, 64
Bennett, Belle Harris, 91
Bentley, Sarah, 91
Bernard of Clairvaux, 31, 32
Bethune, Mary McLeod, 40, 63, 63, 93
Blackwell, Antoinette Brown. See Brown
Blanchard, Jane, 105
Bokenham, Osbern, 28
Booker, Marjorie Leeper, 64
Booth, Catherine, 38, 67, 67, 70, 109
Booth, Evangeline C., 109

Booth, Maud Ballington, 9
Booth, William, 38, 38
Bonaventure, 29
Bowser, Mary Eleanor, 73
Bradstreet, Anne, 40, 46, 47
Bridget of Sweden, 16, 30, 35
Briscoe, Jill, 15
Brown, Antoinette, 53, 82, 82
Brown, Nan M., 64
Brown, Olympia, 106, 106, 106, 106, 106
Bunyan, Elizabeth, 66
Burroughs, Nannie, 62

Calvin, Idelette de Bure, 15, 35, 56
Calvin, John, 36, 37, 37, 37, 37
Cameron, Donaldina, 98
Cannon, Katie G., 64
Carey, Mrs. William, 76
Carey, Mary, 73
Carr, Ann, 69
Cary, Elizabeth, 68
Catherine of Genoa, 77
Catherine of Ricci, 16
Catherine of Siena, 16, 27, 27, 28, 35, 77
Chace, Elizabeth Buffum, 99, 102
Chappell, Winifred L., 93
Chevers, Sarah, 99
Child, Lydia Maria, 109
Chrysotom, 18, 19
Clare, 28, 77
Clement of Alexandria, 7, 23
Clifford, Hettie Rowntree, 73

Cobb, Alice Culler, 94
Coke, Mrs., 91
Collson, Mary, 81, 81
Cooper, Julia, 3
Crosby, Fanny, 9, 107, 107
Crosby, Sarah, 91
Culler (White), Mary, 93
Cushing, Ellen Winsor, 73

Daly, Mary, 7
Day, Dorothy, 2, 5, 9, 40, 76, 76, 78, 78
Delk, Yvonne V., 64
Dillard, Annie, 40
Dix, Dorothea, 109
Dora, Sister, 9
Dutton, Anne, 48
Dyer, Mary, 99

Edburga of Winchester, 26
Eddy, Mary Baker, 5, 40, 80, 80, 80, 81, 81
Edwards, Jonathan, 38
Edwards, Sarah, 15, 38
Egan, Sister Joques, 14
Egeria, 20, 24
Elaw, Zilpha, 61
Eliot, George, 53
Elizabeth of Schonau, 34
Emerson, Ralph Waldo, 46
Ernst, Anna Catharina, 94
Eudokia, 24
Evans, Katherine, 99

Fell, Mary, 99
Fell, Margaret, 99, 99, 100, 101, 102
Finney, Charles, 52
Fleming, Lulu, 75
Fletcher, Mary, 15, 87, 91, 91
Flexner, Helen Thomas, 102
Foote, Julia A. J., 61
Fox, Caroline, 102
Fox, George, 99
Fox, Margaret, 100
Francis of Assisi, 28
Fry, A, Ruth, 102
Fry, Elizabeth, 102, 102

Garrett, Eliza, 87
Garrettson, Katherine Livingston, 87
Gaskell, Elizabeth, 53
Gaunt, Elizabeth, 66, 73
Gladden, Washington, 51
Goldman, Emma, 40
Graham, Isabella, 107
Green, Patricia, 14
Grimke, Angelina, 49, 51, 51, 54, 107
Grimke, Sarah, 7, 49, 51, 107
Gurney, Marion (Mother Marianne of Jesus) 76
Guyon, Jeanne, 29

Haddon, Elizabeth, 99
Hadewijch of Antwerp, 26, 29
Hadewijch of Brabant, 26
de Hailes, Lydia Mary, 73
Harkness, Georgia, 40, 57, 93
Havens, Teresina R., 102
Havergal, Frances Ridley, 9
Hawkes, Daphne, 14
Hawthorne, Nathaniel, 46
Hayes, Lucy Webb, 87
Haygood, Laura Askew, 87
Hazzard, Dorothy, 73
Heck, Barbara, 93
Heloise, 12, 24, 28, 29, 34
Heyrick, Elisabeth, 69
Hildegard of Bingen, 25, 26, 28, 28, 29, 34, 35
Hooten, Elizabeth, 101
Houselander, Caryll, 12, 79, 79
Howe, Julia Ward, 40
Hummer, Catherine, 40
Hunter, Nora S., 82
Huntingdon, Lady, 69, 70, 87, 91, 93
Hutchinson, Anne, 5, 9, 40, 40, 42, 43, 43, 44, 44, 44, 44, 44, 44, 45, 45, 46, 46, 46, 46, 47, 47, 48, 49, 49

Ignatius Loyola, 23, 33
Inskip, Martha, 87

Jackson, Rebecca Cox, 63, 63, 105, 105
Jerome, 7, 11, 18, 21, 24

Joan of Arc, 6, 16, 25, 25, 28, 32, 33, 34, 35
Johnson, Suzan D., 64
Judson, Adoniram, 72
Judson, Ann, 40, 73, 73, 73, 75
Julian of Norwich, 7, 12, 25, 26, 29, 35, 77

Kateri, 71
Kempe, Margery, 7, 25, 26, 27, 27, 35, 35
Kennedy, Minnie, 60
Knight, Carolyn Ann, 64
Knox, John, 11
Knox, Marjorie Bowes, 35
Kruger, Alice, 40
Kubler-Ross, Elisabeth, 40
Kuhlman, Kathryn, 57, 58

LaBerge, Mrs, Agnes N. O., 96
Lanyer, Aemilia, 69
Lathrop, Rose Hawthorne (Mother Alphonsa), 76
Lee, Ann, 5, 7, 40, 103, 103, 104, 105, 105
Lee, Jarena, 3, 61, 64, 90
Lestonnac, Jane, 16
Lewter-Simmons, Margrie, 64
Lincoln, Salome, 73
Lindheim, Irma, 40
Lisle, Lady, 66
Liutgard of Tongern, 34
Logacheva, Anastasiia, 83.
Lovell, Lucy Buffum, 99.
Luder (Luther), Hanna, 38
Luther, Katherine von Bora, 15, 35, 37, 38, 38, 56
Luther, Martin, 7, 37, 38, 38, 38, 38, 38
Lyon, Mary, 51, 51

McGill-Jackson, Deborah, 64
McPherson, Aimee Semple, 40, 58, 58, 60
Macrina, 20
Margaret of Cortona, 32
Mariana de Jesus, 78

Marshall, Catherine, 15
Marshman, Hannah, 73
Mary of Ognies, 34
Mather, Cotton, 47, 47
Maxwell, Lady, 91
Mechthild of Magdeburg, 25, 26, 26, 34, 35, 77
Melania the Younger, 18, 22
Meyer, Lucy Rider, 88, 89
Mills-Bradford, Clara, 64
Milton, John, 7
Monica, 19
Montgomery, Helen Barrett, 72, 73, 74, 75
Moody, Dwight, 38
Moody, Emma, 15, 38
Moon, Lottie (Charlote Diggs), 53, 72
More, Hannah, 53, 70, 70
Morgan, Robin, 40
Mott, Lucretia, 9, 14, 101
Mundy, John, 31
Murray, Grace, 91

Nation, Carrie A., 40, 109
Nichols, Mary Gove, 101
Nietzsche, 11
Nightingale, Florence, 39
Nogarola, Isotta, 30
Noyes, John Humphrey, 7

Oi, Florence Li Tim, 66
Osborn, Sarah, 40

Palladius, 22
Palmer, Phoebe, 40, 90, 90, 92, 92, 93, 93, 97
Pawson, Frances, 91
Peale, Ruth, 15
Peabody, Lucy Waterbury, 72
Penington, Mary, 102
Penn, Hannah, 100
Perot, Rebecca, 63
Perpetua, 12, 28
Peter, Sarah Worthington King, 76
Piccard, Jeannette, 14
Polycarp, 23
Polyxena, 22

Popova, Matrona Naumovna, 83
Porete, Marguerite, 26, 28, 35
Prentiss, Elizabeth, 54
Prior, Margaret, 89

Ramabai Dongre Medlavi, 9, 9
Rauschenbusch, Walter, 51
Renee of France, 36
Ripley, Sophia Dana, 76
Rogers, Hester Ann Roe, 91
Roper, Margaret More, 71
Rosa of Lima, 78
Rufinus, 21

Sale, Elizabeth, 73
Sasso, Rabbi Sandy, 14
Sayers, Dorothy, 6
Schleiermacher, Friedrich, 7
Scott, Peggy R., 64
Segale, Sister Blandina, 12
Seton, Elizabeth Ann, 9, 40, 76, 76
Sexton, Lydia, 106
Shamana, Beverly J., 64
Shaw, Anna Howard, 109
Shuck, Henrietta Hall, 73, 73
Sinclair, Laura, 64
Simpson, Margaret, 15
Smith, Amanda Berry, 40, 64, 65
Smith, Daisy, 15
Smith, Hannah Whitall, 9, 40, 99, 101, 102
Smith, Lucy (Mother Catherine de Ricci), 76
Smith, Martha Hazeltine, 55
Sojourner Truth, 14, 40, 40, 62, 64, 65
Spurgeon, Susannah, 15
Stanton, Elizabeth Cady, 7, 40, 49, 55
Steele, Anne, 73
Stephen, Caroline, 102
Steward, Maria, 3
Stone, Lucy, 53, 55
Stowe, Harriet Beecher, 46, 53

Taisiia, Abbess, 83
Teresa of Avila, 12, 16, 27, 32, 33, 34, 34, 77

Teresa, Mother, 77, 78, 78
Tertullian, 11, 23
Therese of Lisieux, 33, 39, 40, 40, 40, 77
Thoburn, Isabella, 93
Tonna, Elizabeth, 53
Trimmer, Sarah, 70
Tubman, Harriet, 62, 62
Tuchkova, Margarita, 83

Underhill, Evelyn, 56, 60

Van Cott, Maggie, 88, 88
Victoria, Queen, 69
Vining, Elizabeth Gray, 102

Waen, Nora, 102
Warren, William F., 94
Webb, Mary, 56, 75
Weld, Angelina Grimke, See Grimke
Weld, Theodore Dwight, 49
Wesley, John, 38, 87, 87, 88, 91, 94
Wesley, Molly, 38
Wesley, Susanna, 6, 9, 15, 87, 88, 89, 91, 92, 93
White, Alma, 97
White, Ellen G., 4, 40, 102, 102, 102
Wilkinson, Jemima, 40, 72
Willard, Emma, 54
Willard, Frances, 40, 93, 94, 108, 108
Williams, Mary, 73
Williams, Sharon E, 64
Winthrop, John, 49
Winthrop, Margaret, 48
Woodworth-Etter, Maria B., 97
Wright, Lucy, 103, 103, 104

Xanthippe, 22

Young, Ann Eliza, 95
Young, Rosa, 65

Zell, Katherine, 15
Zwingli, Anna Reinhard, 35

*Women in Christian History. A Bibliography.*
compiled and edited by Carolyn DeArmond Blevins.

Mercer University Press, Macon GA 31210-3960.
Isbn 0-86554-493-X. Catalog and warehouse pick number MUP/H387.
Text, interior, and cover designed, and camera-ready pages and cover
    composed by Edd Rowell on a Gateway 2000
        via WordPerfect wp/5.1 and wpwin/5.1/5.2/6.0
        and printed on a LaserMaster 1000.
Text font: (Adobe) Garamond 11/13 and 10/12.
    Display font: Helvetica. Cover titles: (Adobe) Present Script.
Printed and bound by Braun-Brumfield, Inc., Ann Arbor MI 48106.
    Printed via offset lithography on 50# Natural Smooth, 500ppi.
    Smyth sewn and cased into Kivar 7 Performa cloth
        printed PMS 336c (12/green + 2/black)
            plus polyester film lamination over standard binder's boards,
            with headbands and matching endleaves.
    Finished books shrinkwrapped in convenient groups,
        bulk packed in 275#-test cartons, and banded on skids.
                                                    [ October 1995 ]